# The Easdale Doctor

# Mary Withall's previous publications

**Non-fiction**
*The Islands that Roofed the World*
*Villages of Northern Argyll*

**Fiction**
The Eisdalsa trilogy
*Beacon on the Shore*
*The Gorse in Bloom*
*Where the Wild Thyme Grows*

also
*Fields of Heather*
*The Poppy Orchard*
*The Flight of the Cormorants*

# The Easdale Doctor

## The Life and Times of Patrick H. Gillies

*Mary Withall*

BIRLINN

First published in 2006 by
Birlinn Limited
West Newington House
10 Newington Road
Edinburgh
EH9 1QS

*www.birlinn.co.uk*
Reprinted 2009

ISBN13: 978 1 84158 437 9

British Library Cataloguing-in-Publication Data
A catalogue record for this book is available from the British Library

Designed and typeset by Wordsense, Edinburgh
Printed and bound by GraphyCems, Spain

# Contents

*Patrick H. Gillies, Bachelor of Medicine, Bachelor of Surgery, Bachelor of Science, Fellow of the Scottish Society of Arts, c.1930.*

# *Preface*

---

THERE IS ONLY one person alive today with first-hand knowledge of Dr Patrick Gillies: his nephew Walter, Dr Wattie Gillies, remembers his uncle Pat from when he himself was a very small child. Being the youngest in a large, well-spread family, Wattie, now in his eighties, can barely remember what his uncle looked like but he recalls vividly the tales his father told him of the family and their life together.

A portrait of Patrick shows him to be of stocky build with a good head of fair hair. This was carefully plastered with macassar oil for the photograph but when it had been newly washed by rain and dried in the wind it was more likely to be sticking up in a fuzzy halo. What the photograph does not indicate is that he was a little under six feet tall and must have been quite a formidable figure. There is little doubt that he was a big man, for his son Alexander was described in the newspapers as being six feet two inches and his grandson, also a Patrick, must be all of that! Only the laughter lines about his eyes give away the truly benign nature of this kindly man.

The portrait shows the doctor to have been a man who preferred comfortable country clothes. Having a portrait taken in a studio even in 1920 was not a casual affair. One wore one's best for the occasion or, as in Patrick's case, what one felt most comfortable in. Patrick did not sport the fashionable black cut-a-way jacket and pinstriped trousers of the rather more self-important members of his profession. As well as being a medical doctor, he was a farmer and proud of it, and, to complete this portrait of a Victorian country gentleman, one feels he could seldom have been seen without a pipe in his mouth. Judging from those of his descendants, his eyes were grey and clear as the winter skies of his beloved Slate Isles. They missed nothing, recording every detail, to be filed away in a well ordered mind, which remained sharp and humorous until the day he died.

I first encountered the work of Dr Patrick Gillies when, during my first long dark winter on Easdale Island, I was asked to transcribe the contents of one of the doctor's letter books, which, having been found in the loft of one of the cottages, had been presented to the Easdale Museum. How the book happened to be there remains a mystery to this day but we are indebted to whoever preserved it. The correspondence, including the doctor's annual reports to the county medical officer, gives a graphic account not only of the ailments but also of the day-to-day living experience of the people of Easdale and the parish of Kilbrandon and Kilchattan.

In what is an exceptionally neat hand for a medical man, Patrick draws a picture of a population of hard-working, skilful men and the womenfolk who fed them, raised their children and kept house in the most difficult of climates. Today we have washing machines and dryers on Easdale Island but the women of Patrick's era hung their washing out to dry in gale-force winds and were lucky if they got it in before the next downpour. Through Patrick's letters and reports we see the steady decline of the slate industry – the sole reason for the existence of such an exceptionally large population in the islands. We also witness the rapid increase in the diseases associated with poverty and overcrowding. The records are a microcosm of human endeavour and endurance.

Patrick's life as the son of a country doctor was never as cushioned as one might perhaps expect. His father died when he was eleven years old and, being the brightest although not the oldest in Dr Hugh Gillies' family, he took upon himself responsibility for his siblings from an early age. From his mother he learnt frugality so that throughout his life he continued to count the bawbees. If, in some of his correspondence, he appears obsessed with demands for a few pennies here and there, it must be remembered that in 1890 sixpence would have bought a meal for a family. As part of a six-strong team, one man's income from making a thousand roofing slates was one-sixth part of a pound sterling.

Patrick rarely fought the authorities on his own behalf but he was vociferous in his demands for a decent life for the working men of his district and in that he might be described as a socialist with a small 's'. Although firmly rooted

University certificate of merit awarded to P.H. Gillies in 1887.

in the politically Liberal, middle-class society from which he sprang, he never suffered fools gladly, particularly amongst his 'ratepayer' neighbours, and in the pursuit of his philanthropic ends he was apt to tread on a few toes.

Recognising his value to their society in general, the parishioners elected him to their school board and their parish council, both bodies of considerable influence at the end of the nineteenth century, and in due course he was invited to become a justice of the peace.

It might be thought that a man with so many commitments would have had little time for literary activities but during the course of his life Patrick gave a number of lectures in both the Gaelic and English languages, wrote numerous articles for learned journals and in 1909 published his history of the Slate Islands, *Netherlorn and its Neighbourhood*. He was preparing another book, on the life of John Campbell, 1st Marquis of Breadalbane, when he died. For his literary achievements he was invited to become a fellow of the Scottish Royal Society of Arts. Added to all this was his not inconsiderable service in the Army in two wars and his work during a total of twenty-three years, with Argyll County Council.

I am indebted to the Gillies family, in particularly Fiona Hamilton, Davinia Ballantyne and Patricia Suvyer, Patrick's granddaughters, for allowing me free access to the family archives and for reading the initial manuscript. They provided several items of unrecorded family lore and made a number of useful suggestions which have added colour to this account of Patrick's life. As always, Murdo McDonald, until lately the archivist of Argyll and Bute Council, was most generous with his time, seeking out obscure references and making my visits to his office always worthwhile. In addition I would like to acknowledge the help given by the curators of the Imperial War Museum, the Museum of the Royal Army Medical Corps and the librarians of both Glasgow and Edinburgh Universities together with staff of the Scottish Records Office. My thanks also to Jean Adams, until lately curator of the Easdale Island Folk Museum, for allowing access to the archives and to the trustees of the Slate Islands Heritage Trust for permission to use photographic material. Finally I would like to thank Hugh Andrew and Andrew Simmons of Birlinn for their encouragement and support and in particular my editor Aline Hill for her observations and many helpful suggestions.

Mary Withall

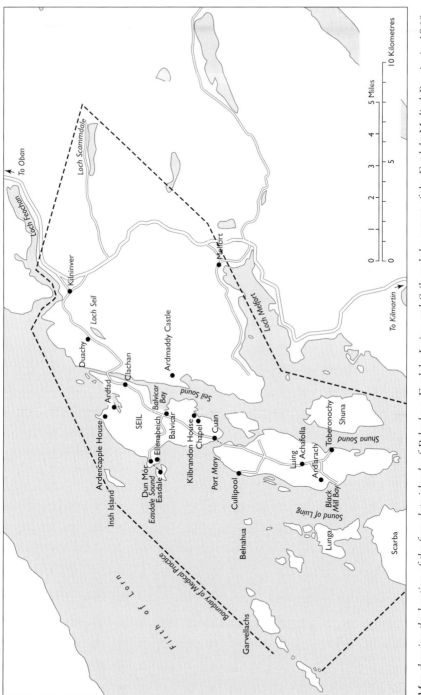

Map showing the location of the four slate islands of Belnahua, Easdale, Luing and Seil, and the extent of the Easdale Medical Practice in 1860. The boundaries have changed little to the present day.

# 1  Roots and Branches

ODAY'S VISITOR TO Argyll, travelling northwards from the Mull of Kintyre
to the more famous tourist attractions of Glen Coe, Fort William and
the Isle of Skye, might well pass, unseeing, the Slate Islands of Netherlorn.
They lie just a few hundred metres off shore in the turbulent Sound of Lorn,
which separates the larger islands of Jura, Scarba and Mull from the mainland
of Argyll. The professional fisherman and the amateur sailor, however, know
these islands well as a place of refuge, and will seek out the sheltered coves and
inlets in a storm just as did the Viking mariners, who came here a thousand
years ago.

The Vikings found here timber for their boats, fodder for their beasts and
meat for the table. They also discovered the uniquely rich bounty of these
islands, a bounty which would eventually make the islands famous throughout the world. Seil and Luing, Belnahua and Easdale are composed largely of
slate, a laminated rock which was laid down as mud six hundred million years
ago. The deposits were compressed, contorted and baked by the massive earth
movements which created the Highlands of Scotland, and transformed into the
hard blue rock which is known to geologists as Easdale Slate.

For many millennia the slate lay exposed to the elements. Its surfaces, crum-
bled by successive frosts and baking sun, were worn smooth by the rivers and
the tides. In time volcanic activity, centred upon the Isle of Mull, spewed lava
outwards in concentric circles covering the rocks that had been denuded by
weathering with sheets of basaltic lava which formed the rock called Andesite.

*Beds of Easdale slate as they appear on Easdale Island, displaying the acute angle of dip which necessitated quarrying to extreme depths below sea level.*

There followed further upheavals which tipped the slate beds over to an angle of approximately thirty-seven degrees and created fissures in the rocks later to be filled with lava after further eruptions of the Mull volcanoes. Throughout the Pleistocene, successive ice ages created raised beaches and shingley shores, many of which were later engulfed when the ice melted. Where sections of the coast have been swamped by the rising sea level, islands of slate rock have been left standing up above the waves, their markedly triangular profiles stark against the western horizon. The Sound of Lorn is dotted with such islands, some of them, like Seil and Luing, are large enough to support a sizeable population, while Easdale and Belnahua, neither of them more than a square mile in area, both supported just a single village. Others again are just small lumps of rock, inhabited only by sea birds and seals.

While volcanoes and ice sheets had in turn a profound effect upon the land-scape of the Slate Islands, the changes subsequently brought about by man's activity are no less important. They resulted from the method of quarrying employed to win the slate rock. Once all the available slate had been removed to sea level, the men began to dig down into the ground following the dip of the tilted slate beds. Over a period of two hundred years or more the quarrying reached depths of as much as seventy metres below sea level. Keeping the quar-

ries dry while the men were working required both ingenuity and perseverance from the engineers who ran the quarries. When work finally ceased at the
beginning of the twentieth century these great pits in the ground quickly filled
with water, creating a landscape dotted with deep, tranquil pools surrounded
by heaps of waste slate.

Today the slate islands present the visitor with a landscape of tranquil beauty.
Even the slate waste is slowly becoming covered by vegetation and in spring
and early summer the blue-grey rocks are splashed with the bright colours of
wild flowers: thyme and thrift; hairbell and lady slipper; stonecrop and ling.

Neolithic Man used slabs of the slate rock for flooring and to cover the cists of
the dead. The Vikings cut and carved the slate slabs into elaborate gravestones,
while the great Scottish warlords of the twelfth and thirteenth centuries used
the rock to roof their castles. Roofing slates were made by splitting the rock
to separate the laminations and trimming the flat, thin sheets into rectangles
which, when laid, overlapping, across a timber roof, made a fine waterproof
covering. So durable are these blue Easdale slates, readily distinguished by their
generous scattering of golden crystals of iron pyrites, that they have remained
unaltered on some buildings for hundreds of years, only the timber that sup-
ports them having to be replaced from time to time.

By the end of the seventeenth century the Earl of Breadalbane and his cousin
the Duke of Argyll, who between them owned most of the county and much
of Perthshire and Stirlingshire besides, began to exploit the slate deposits on a
commercial basis and in 1745 a company was formally registered, the Easdale
Marble and Slate Quarrying Company. Villages were built to accommodate
the influx of workers and because of the dangerous nature of the work a surgeon was appointed to minister to the men and their families.

It was into this environment that Patrick Hunter Gillies was born, the son of
a country doctor, in 1869 in the tiny township of Caolas at the most westerly
point of the Isle of Seil. The settlement was at the time composed of a few
cottages gathered around the tiny harbour of Easdale and overshadowed by the
towering cliffs of Ben Mor. While Caolas itself had been settled from earliest
times, in the first two decades of the nineteenth century the village had been
enlarged to accommodate a growing population of quarry workers. The quarrymen and their families were housed in three rows of terraced, whitewashed

cottages whose harled stone walls and slated roofs were a match for anything the elements might send against them. In winter these houses are swept by gales from the north and west and the shores beside them are pounded by the Atlantic Ocean. In summer the winds veer to the south-west bringing more gentle rain and calmer seas but the warmer weather is accompanied by the mighty Highland midge, today the scourge of holidaymakers but once the bane of those obliged to carry on their work amongst clouds of the tiny marauders in the early morning and as the day drew to a close!

A hundred and fifty metres off shore, the island of Easdale sported a fine harbour of its own and a village of quarry workers' houses which had been built a quarter of a century earlier than those on Seil. Easdale Island accommodated some four hundred and fifty people in 1870 while the population of Easdale Village on Seil was around three hundred. Because the whole district was called Easdale, the two settlements came to be known as the Island and the Village, and, although the manager of the quarries was responsible for the work of both, the inhabitants set themselves apart from one another as though they might be two different nations. Should a girl from the Island marry a man from the Village she was waved off from her home island on her wedding day as though she were going to a faraway, foreign land.

*Caolas, the township on the north shore of Ellenabeich harbour, as it is today. Several of the houses were already in place in 1863 when Dr Hugh Gillies arrived in Easdale.*

The proximity of the sea and the presence of two sheltered harbours separated by a sound deep enough to allow the passage and mooring of large coastal vessels allowed Easdale to become an important port of call along the west coast. A fine wooden pier was constructed at Easdale Village on Seil in the 1870s to accommodate passenger- and cargo-carrying steamers, and the villagers travelled regularly by sea, north to Oban and Inverness and south to Crinan and Glasgow. By contrast, the roads were for the most part unmetalled, pot-holed and unsuitable for traffic other than the occasional farm cart, pony trap or horseman.

Ships came from far afield to Easdale in order to carry away the slates manufactured in the slate villages. First it was Glasgow and the burgeoning cities of

Aerial view of Ellenabeich. The three rows of quarriers' cottages with their two narrow streets are clearly visible. Easdale Island, with its excellent harbour and ancient cottages, some built as early as 1770, lies 120 metres off shore. The large quarry to the west of Ellenabeich Village was breached during the storm of November 1881 and has remained flooded ever since. What was once the Island of Birches was quarried away, waste slate being dumped in the narrow channel between the island and Caolas on Seil Island. On this man-made ground quarrymen's cottages were erected in the 1820s.

the east coast of Scotland – Inverness, Aberdeen, Dundee and Edinburgh – that created a demand. Later, orders came from England and Ireland, the east-coast cities of the Americas, the West Indies, the Baltic states and even Australia and New Zealand. For the young Patrick Gillies and his siblings it was an education in itself simply to wander along the quay, listening to the talk of sailors from around the world, come to this unlikely port of call to buy their supplies of slate. It was in this cosmopolitan atmosphere that Patrick the boy grew up into the man he was, his mind ever open to new ideas and looking always beyond the horizon to new adventures and fresh challenges.

While the coastal villages of Seil and Easdale together with those on the adjoining Slate Islands of Luing and Belnahua were engaged from dawn until dusk in heavy industry, creating both noise and dust, the countryside all around remained apparently untouched by this activity.

In addition to their slate deposits, the Slate Islands of Netherlorn are comprised of high ridges of hard volcanic rock covered in gorse and heather. The steeper slopes are grazed by sheep while the deep narrow valleys between are fertile pockets of lush grasses where cattle may graze and where grain and flax may be grown.

Today the hillsides are covered in dark, monotonous swathes of Canadian and Scandinavian pines, planted in the mid-twentieth century, but when Patrick was a young lad, roaming the hills with his brothers, the woodlands he explored were ancient oakwoods and coppices of ash and alder abundant with wildlife which might be hunted or trapped, provided His Lordship's gillies were nowhere in the offing. The numerous burns and lochans abounded in salmon and sea trout and, like all the lads of his generation, Patrick learned early how to angle for these elusive fish. He spent many hours in quiet solitude, observing the wild creatures around him. These early roamings gave him an intimate knowledge of the countryside surrounding his home and led him in later years to write in vivid terms about Netherlorn and its neighbourhood. His parents' various servants and the villagers with whom the boy Patrick mingled had a rich store of folktales which they shared with him and which he later remembered in his writings and lectures.

Although while in school Patrick and his siblings were obliged to speak and write English, his mother's house servants and his father's patients for the most part spoke Gaelic. Patrick himself became fluent in both languages and was able throughout his life to communicate freely in either.

*Patrick Gillies aged 6, c.1875.*　　　　　*Patrick's brother Hugh aged 10, c.1880.*

Patrick's early days were spent in close contact with the families of fishermen and agricultural workers as well as those of the quarrymen. Because of his father's position as one of the few professional men in the district, Patrick was also at ease amongst the families of the tenant farmers, of the minister, the local lawyer and even that of the Marquis of Breadalbane himself whose country seat was Ardmaddy Castle, situated on the Argyll mainland but within the bounds of his father's medical practice. Thus, in complete contrast with the majority of the middle classes of the day, Patrick was able to bridge the gap between master and servant, rich and poor, and because he was, above all things, a compassionate human being, he was never backward in furthering the interests of his working-class neighbours.

From the day he was born, Patrick Gillies was destined to become one of the outstanding medical men of his day but his other interests in many ways eclipsed his medical prowess, phenomenal though this was. An unusual combination of social awareness, aestheticism, literary aptitude and scientific expertise led him along a number of different pathways where he seems to have excelled in whatever task he undertook. It was his rugged determination to do right, his kindness in the adversity of others and his resilience during his own times of trial, which endeared him to those who knew him best. His strong sense of humour, his deep understanding of the human psyche and his great spirit of adventure created a colourful background against which to display his works. A glance into his ancestry tells us a great deal about the remarkable gene pool from which Patrick Hunter Gillies emerged.

Like so many Scottish families the Gillies are able to trace their ancestry back to the times when there were no surnames, when a man was known by what he did for a living or by some feat achieved on the field of battle. Succeeding generations then took the name of the father. Mac, the son of, precedes many a Scottish family name. A gillie was, and is, a gamekeeper, the man who tends the game birds and animals and protects the stock on his master's lands, keeping at bay those who might seek to steal it. One may imagine therefore that within Patrick's genes there existed an inborn capacity for appreciation and deep understanding of the countryside, which manifested itself in later years in his written accounts of the district in which he lived.

Mr Jack McIntyre of Royston, Herts, has traced the family tree back as far as 1514, to Eogan of Glenmore on the Isle of Skye. A second early ancestor was Donald Mhor (Donald the Great, or Big), who died in 1630. The first mention of anyone of the name of Gillies is in a sasine of 1667 in which one Donald Gillies of Durcha is said to have held land in Argyll. There is little doubt that Patrick's ancestors originated in Ireland and were among those Scotti who accompanied to Argyll the Irish priests of the sixth century, such as Brendon of Clonfert and Kattan, who gave their names to the Slate Islands parishes of Kilbrandon and Kilchattan, and Columba, who first built a settlement on Eilean Naomin, the most westerly of the Garvellach islands in the Sound of Lorn, before travelling on to set up his more famous abbey on Iona.

For many generations the Gillies family held tenancy in Kilmartin Glen, to the north of the village of Kilmartin in Argyll, beneath the walls of Carnasserie Castle and it was here that Patrick's father, Hugh Gillies, was born in 1836, the youngest son of John Gillies, one-time tenant of Auchoist Farm, Lochgilphead and tacksman to the Duke of Argyll. Despite his own farming background, John Gillies was not slow to recognise scholarly potential in at least two of his nine children, encouraging them to study for a profession. In this he was assisted by his brother, also Hugh, the schoolmaster at the nearby village of Kilmichael Glassary. Thus it was that Hugh Gillies' brother, Alexander, eight years his senior, studied medicine and emigrated to Australia in the 1850s. There he began his own dynasty of Gillies doctors, which included Malcolm Gillies, one of the founders of the town of Bowen in Queensland. Hugh also chose to study medicine rather than either the ministry or law and at the age of eighteen entered his name on the roll of students at the Andersonian University of Glasgow from whence he graduated with honours in both surgery and physic in 1859 at the age of twenty-three years. Unlike many students of his day he did not engage in wild behaviour but spent his time studying diligently, as his professors observed; R. Newton MD, Professor of Surgery testified that he 'conducted himself throughout in the most exemplary manner', while James MacShie MD, Superintendent of the Glasgow Royal Infirmary wrote 'In all respects he has proved himself to be a man of diligent and industrious habits and is well qualified for the exercise of his profession.'

Rather surprisingly for those days, Hugh also obtained a diploma in midwifery, which was to stand him in good stead in his work amongst the well-populated quarry villages of the Slate Islands. Hugh's first post as a medical practitioner was in the parish of Glenorchy and Inishail, which surrounds the eastern end of Loch Awe and stretches as far east as Tyndrum. Although the principal village is Dalmally, Hugh's practice covered also the more remote regions of Glenorchy, Glen Shae and the surrounding mountains. Home visits required the doctor to travel great distances, either on foot or on horseback, often in the foulest weather. Appointed by the Earl of Breadalbane on the recommendation of his professors, Hugh spent two-and-a-half years amongst the people of Glenorchy before transferring, at the request of His Lordship, to the slate quarrying Easdale District of Netherlorn. So highly was Hugh's work valued in Glenorchy that his patients, dismayed by his proposed departure, raised a petition carrying one hundred names begging him to remain. His Lordship's wishes prevailed however, and when Hugh eventually left the district he was showered with gifts and messages of goodwill. So high was his standing in this community that at his untimely death, some twenty years later, the parishioners of Glenorchy insisted upon being included in the subscription list for Hugh's memorial.

There is little doubt that Hugh Gillies was already familiar with the quarrying villages of the Slate Islands before he came there to settle in the year 1863.

There were members of the Gillies family, albeit distant cousins, already established on the islands of Luing and Belnahua and there was a good deal of movement, intermarriage and business association between the various branches. As a bachelor, it is likely Hugh lodged first of all with one of these relatives before he obtained the lease on a small house at Caolas.

The medical practice to which Hugh Gillies came in 1863 was much the same in extent as is the Easdale practice today. In the south it was bounded by the village of Kilmelford and the south-eastern shore of the Degnish peninsula. At Kilmelford, there was a gunpowder mill employing a large number of men, and numerous calls were made on the doctor's services from the gunpowder workers and their families. The peninsula of Degnish is bisected by a ridge of high ground supporting little but grazing for sheep and, on the lower slopes, woodland, which in those days provided the charcoal essential for the manufacture of gunpowder and to a lesser extent in the operation of the slate quarries.

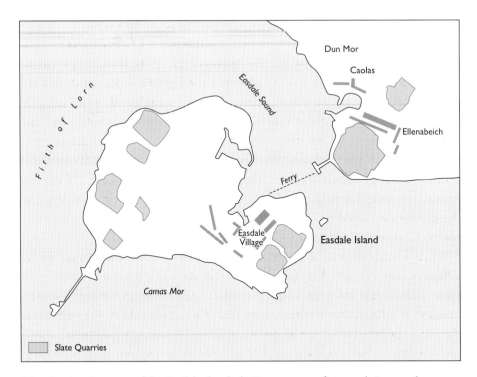

*Map showing the extent of the Easdale slate beds. Outcrops occur from north Jura northeastwards at intervals along the line of the Great Glen fault, but only at Easdale and Ballachulish were the slates quarried extensively on a commercial basis.*

Facing north-west across Balvicar Sound is Ardmaddy Castle, at that time the country seat of the Earl of Breadalbane. When the nobleman's family was in residence, the doctor paid frequent visits to the castle to attend His Lordship, his family and members of his staff. To the east, the practice extended as far as the village of Kilmore at the eastern end of Loch Feochan, and the north shore of the loch formed the northern boundary of the doctor's territory.

The major part of the practice however lay amongst the Slate Islands of Seil, Luing, Easdale and Belnahua, and a number of smaller inhabited islands such as Lunga and Torsa. Although, particularly on Luing and Seil, there was a substantial population engaged in agricultural activities, the greatest numbers worked in the slate quarries, the villages being ranged around the more prolific quarries of Easdale Island, Easdale Village and Balvicar on Seil, Toberonochy and Cullipool on Luing and the island of Belnahua where more than one third of the island had been dug away to provide roofing slates for the developing town of Oban.

In 1863 the quarries were at the peak of their output, producing as many as nine million slates a year and exporting them around the globe. Night and day the air would have been filled with the constant beat of the water pumps removing rainwater and seawater which had seeped through the rocks, hampering the quarrying operations. By this date most of the quarries had been hollowed out to more than a hundred feet below sea level. During daylight hours the pumps were joined by the steady tap-tapping of the slate cutters' hammers as they worked away in their tiny makeshift shelters to the accompaniment of the squeaking and groaning of the winding gear hauling ton upon ton of rock to the surface. And, like the big base drum in the orchestra, at intervals throughout the day the air would be rent by explosions as a wall of rock was blasted away somewhere deep below sea level.

When Hugh Gillies arrived to take up his new job, Easdale Island and the village of Easdale on Seil each sustained a population of four hundred and fifty men, women and children, while in total the population of the parish of Kilbrandon and Kilchattan boasted nearly three thousand souls. At the same time, the entire population of the adjoining parish of Kilmore and Kilbride, which included the Burgh of Oban, amounted to less than two thousand.

The imposition of so large a body of people upon such a remote, not to say forbidding, environment placed upon the Easdale Quarrying Company certain obligations towards its workforce. Seeing the importance of maintaining a contented and healthy community, in addition to providing medical cover for the men and their families the Quarrying Company provided schools for the children and a company store to ensure that the men and their families were well catered for in good times and bad.

An important innovation was the introduction of a medical insurance scheme which ensured that no family would suffer unduly if the breadwinner was injured or taken ill as a result of his work. At the cost of a few shillings a year the quarrymen were guaranteed medical attendance for themselves and their families; only confinements and certain items of surgical apparatus were charged for. This was an excellent scheme from the doctor's point of view as well since it provided a guaranteed source of income which he was able to augment with fees from his private practice, the difference here being that whereas the men's contributions were automatically deducted from their wages every payday, Hugh's private patients were often reluctant to settle their doctor's bills until forced to do so.

The major landowner in the district was the Earl of Breadalbane himself, and most land and property was leased from him. Once he had settled in Caolas, Hugh negotiated the lease of a small house where he was to spend his first nine years in the practice. At this time a professional gentleman would expect to augment his income from the proceeds of the policies surrounding his house. Unfortunately Hugh's tenancy at Caolas did not include any cultivable land. At Dunmore, on the outskirts of the village, the substantial Dunmore House was occupied by the leaseholder of the quarries, a Mr Bett from Glasgow. Mr Bett had no interest in working the farm which was attached to Dunmore House and was pleased to sublet the farm buildings and loch to the new doctor. Unable to work the land himself on a regular basis, Hugh was obliged to install a farm manager in the farmhouse, but was nevertheless able to draw a substantial additional income from this investment.

Among the first people with whom Hugh became intimately acquainted was John Whyte, the manager of the Easdale Quarries. Born in Dalmally, the son of a farm labourer, John had benefited from the Earl of Breadalbane's policy of nurturing the talent found amongst his own people. By providing the most able with education and training, His Lordship was able to procure a substantial, well-equipped workforce with which to operate his vast estates, and his benevolence procured the loyalty of employees and tenants alike. Most of the earl's professional appointees, lawyers, clergymen and doctors were from among his own people. Although there is no evidence to prove it there is every likelihood that Hugh Gillies had also benefited from Breadalbane's patronage.

John Whyte, a pupil gifted in mathematics and sciences, was encouraged to stay on at school until, at the age of fifteen, he took an apprenticeship with a firm of mining engineers. His apprenticeship completed, he was appointed to the Easdale quarries in 1842, the year John Campbell, nephew of the 16th Earl of Breadalbane, succeeded to the title. The new earl had spent much of his childhood at Ardmaddy where his father was the captain of the castle and acted as the earl's agent in the district. As a child John Campbell had played with the village children and many of the quarry workers at the time of his succession were his childhood friends. By 1863 when Hugh Gillies arrived to take up his medical duties, the earl and the engineer had improved the operation of the quarries to new heights of efficiency and the increased output promised to ensure a prosperous future for everyone. The appearance upon the scene of a young, imaginative and well-qualified doctor completed the trio which, acting in unison, looked set to improve even further the everyday lives of the slate workers.

John Whyte and Hugh Gillies became firm friends and enthusiastic colleagues, while the relationship of both men with the earl was always warm and friendly. John Whyte exhibited a degree of social conscience, rare amongst employers of the time. Hugh's natural instinct was to support the weak and oppressed. Concerned that boys of eleven years of age were starting work in the quarries only half educated, the two men provided evening classes to improve the workers' knowledge of mathematics, science, engineering and the English language. With the help of the parish minister and occasional visiting speakers, they themselves provided the teaching and the Easdale Technical Institute was established. Although it faltered occasionally, at times when the industry was in difficulties, the institute survived into the early years of the twentieth century.

The local form of communication was Gaelic but John Whyte, observing the difficulties experienced in the quarries whenever he brought in extra labour from Lowland Scotland and across the Border, decided that the language of communication in the quarries should be English. Anxious to gain a command of the language, many older men joined the evening classes in English and stayed on to improve their general knowledge of engineering and science. In the 1870s, with the introduction of the Education (Scotland) Act of 1872, English became the language of the schoolroom and for many years the use of

Gaelic, even in the school yard, was strictly forbidden. As a consequence of this sadly misjudged solution to a problem which might have been resolved by less Draconian means, there are very few Gaelic speakers in Easdale District today, despite recent valiant attempts by primary schools to rectify the error.

At this prosperous period for the slate industry, Hugh Gillies' daily round was largely restricted to attending accident cases in the quarries and the Melfort powder works and the confinements of the wives of the working men. The diseases of poverty and neglect, poor sanitation and inadequate housing found amongst the agricultural workers were hardly ever found in the quarry villages. Reported cases of cholera, enteric fever (typhoid) and tuberculosis were rare.

Little more than a year after Hugh came to Easdale the happy association between John Campbell, 16th Earl of Breadalbane, and his two friends came to an abrupt end when the earl died suddenly at his family seat of Taymouth Castle. The accession of Gavin Campbell, 17th Earl of Breadalbane, was to bring great changes to the Easdale quarrying community. Gavin, unlike his predecessor, took little personal interest in the quarries and was content to lease them to a group of Glasgow businessmen who had interests in the construction industry. These gentlemen, concerned only to produce the largest number of slates for the least financial investment, took little interest in the welfare of their workforce and, with a steady reduction of investment in new equipment, conditions in the quarries became even more dangerous. Hugh's workload grew by leaps and bounds as the number and severity of the accidents increased. No longer were the dependents of injured men and the widows of those killed taken care of by the company and, for the first time, quarry workers' families began to seek help from the parish council.

Both Hugh Gillies and John Whyte were, by virtue of their position in the community, members of the parish council and it was their job to administer the Poor Law. John Whyte, unable to look on while the organisation that he and John Campbell had so painstakingly created, was slowly destroyed, resigned his post and moved to another position on the east coast, leaving behind his eldest son, Angus, as master of the Easdale Quarries. Angus, just a year or two younger than Hugh, took his father's place as the doctor's colleague and the two men were to work side by side for nearly twenty years, attempting to stay the decline which had been so thoughtlessly inspired by the new lessees.

Hugh Gillies remained a bachelor for another three years before marrying Janet Hunter, a farmer's daughter from the parish of Aberlemno in Inverness-shire. This was a happy choice of bride by the young doctor for Janet, or Jessie Hunter as she was known amongst her friends and family, was an independent young woman, well schooled in the skills and duties of a farmer's daughter. Tall and elegant, she commanded the respect and admiration of the community, effectively gracing the doctor's position in the parish. A 'modern' woman in every sense, she was both intelligent and resourceful. It was she who persuaded Hugh to remain at Caolas until a house became available which had its own farm attached. With such a competent farmer for a wife, Hugh no longer needed to employ a farm manager to run his present agricultural interests. Jessie herself, with the help of a couple of labourers, now undertook the management of the farm at Dunmore.

With Hugh totally absorbed in his medical work and his dealings with the parish council and Jessie having a free hand with the farm, the couple settled down, happily looking forward to the birth of their first child. There was no doubt that the house at Caolas, although large enough to accommodate the medical

practice and Hugh and Jessie on their own, was not going to be suitable for a family. Within weeks of becoming pregnant with her first child, Jessie began looking for a more suitable house.

Their ownership of the lease on Dunmore Farm restricted their choice of an alternative house since it would be impractical for them to live at any great distance from the farm and the livestock. The only realistic place for them to live was Dunmore House itself but

*Jessie Gillies, Patrick's mother (seated), with her daughter Janet (also Jessie) and a family friend, 1880s.*

A view of Dunmore Farm meadow. The road linking Balvicar and Ellenabeich runs beside the shore where the Gillies doctors kept their boat ready for emergency calls. Turnips and kale were grown as fodder for the stock on part of the ground. The remainder was cultivated for hay, the crops being rotated to conserve the quality of the soil.

unfortunately Mr Bett seemed set to remain where he was for many years to come! He had not however reckoned with the force of Cupid's arrow. During a visit to the doctor's home at Caolas, Jessie's sister, Elizabeth Hunter, chanced to meet Mr Bett at a social gathering in the village hall. The apparently confirmed bachelor from Glasgow had so far managed to avoid the snares of city society and had been quite unmoved by the charms of those unmarried daughters who were paraded before him in the more fashionable city drawing rooms. Under the spell of a moonlit Easdale night however, Mr Bett fell in love with Liza Hunter and within a few short weeks he had plighted his troth and been accepted. The couple were married soon after and Liza moved into the grand house which her sister coveted.

Although born to life on an Inverness-shire farm, Liza had no interest in the land and lacked entirely any of her sister's farming instincts. She had spent her girlhood longing for the bright lights and had her heart set upon moving to Mr Bett's Glasgow residence as soon as possible. From the start she was determined that her husband should be persuaded to give up his tenancy at Easdale and move back to his Glasgow residence from where he would be able

Dunmore House as it appears today. To the left is the eighteenth-century portion of the building, which was extended in the early nineteenth century. Twentieth-century additions are out of sight at the rear. The fenestration is largely unaltered, although some of the Georgian panes have been replaced by larger sheets of glass. Some older panes bear signatures inscribed by the Gillies children, presumably using someone's diamond ring!

to conduct his business equally well. Unable to deny his new bride anything, when in 1873 the time came to renew his lease, Bett relinquished his tenancy. With prior knowledge of his brother-in-law's intentions, Hugh Gillies wasted no time in approaching Breadalbane's agent with his bid for the tenancy and Jessie's joy was unbounded when he finally signed a twelve-year lease for both house and farm.

With three children already and another on the way, the move was none too soon so far as Jessie was concerned. Her first son, John, had been born in the house at Caolas in 1867, towards the end of the Gillies' first year of marriage. In two years, Patrick Hunter Gillies had arrived on the scene to be followed, one year later, by his brother Hugh. To help her with the household chores and to take care of the children, Jessie hired a servant from the village. This lady, steeped in the folklore and history of Lorn, was the source of much of the young Patrick's knowledge of the history of the area. Miss Campbell was a Gaelic speaker and it was in this language that the children in her charge first learnt to speak. Thus it was that by the time they went to the village school all the Gillies

children were bilingual. Both Patrick and Hugh remained fluent in both spoken and written Gaelic throughout their lives.

The doctor's family finally moved into Dunmore House in the late summer of 1873, the year that Patrick Hunter Gillies started school. It was to remain the family home for the next forty years.

*Dr Hugh Gillies, Patrick's father, c.1880. Hugh was medical officer to the Easdale Slate Quarrying Company from 1859 until his early death in 1880.*

Dunmore proved to be the perfect location for the doctor's residence. The house was of eighteenth-century construction under a gabled and slated roof, and was of substantial proportions, having a number of large public rooms as well as sufficient bedrooms to accommodate the family, which had recently increased to four on the arrival three months before of a daughter, Janet (later called Jessie like her mother). To Jessie's delight the very large farmhouse kitchen was augmented by a dairy of sufficient proportions to allow for a small commercial enterprise.

Situated within easy distance from Easdale village and the quarries on Easdale Island, the property had its own stretch of shoreline where the doctor could moor a boat to take him to the nearby islands within his practice. The house was two miles from Balvicar village where crossroads gave access to all parts of the Slate Islands either, by sea or over land. The house was three miles by road from the new parish church of Kilbrandon on the Cuan road although it is most likely the family walked to church on a Sunday by way of the shortcut over Smithy Brae and past the ancient hill-fort of Cnoc an Tighe Mhoir. The villages of Clachan and Kilmelford were easily accessed by pony trap or on horseback, by way of hill tracks, while Ardmaddy Castle could be reached by use of ferry boat from Balvicar.

The farm proved ideal for Jessie's purposes. There was grazing for some two hundred sheep and a small herd of dairy cattle while the valley floor supported crops of grain and winter fodder for the beasts. Turnips and kale, potatoes and other root vegetables were grown to feed both the family and the animals. The milk was sold locally as were the cheese and butter which Jessie herself made in the dairy. Further up the glen there were two small steadings called Cairnban and an Grianan, which were held by sub-

*The older parts of Dunmore House remain much as they were in the 1880s. The delicate balustrade and very fine plaster cornices are typical of building standards of the late eighteenth and early nineteenth century.*

tenants who were available to help out on the main farm when needed.

John Gillies, Hugh and Jessie's first born, was never a willing scholar. Even when a schoolboy he was far happier helping out around the farm or out fishing with the men from the village than he was confined to the schoolroom. He left the village school at the first opportunity and began to work full-time on the family farm.

Patrick, on the other hand, showed from an early age a quick intelligence and a prodigious memory for detail. Within a few short years he had become his father's constant companion, accompanying him on his rounds and familiarising himself with much of the difficult terminology of the physician. Perhaps more importantly, at this stage in his development he became familiar with the whole range of the human condition, joining Hugh on his visits to both the richest and poorest homes in the neighbourhood. Patrick cannot have failed to notice his father's manner in dealing with his patients for Hugh Gillies treated everyone, whether it was the earl in his castle or the lonely widow in her dismal bothy, with an equal degree of concern and courtesy. In his social dealings with the parishioners, the good doctor was as content to drink a tankard of ale with quarrymen in the Tigh an Truish Inn as he was to sip Madeira wine in Her Ladyship's boudoir. He and Jessie were as comfortable joining in the singing and dancing at a ceilidh in the village as they were listening to a string quartet in the castle ballroom.

As he grew older, Patrick was to adhere always to his father's principles of benevolence and compassion, but this legacy of social awareness was tempered by a frugality and practicality which must be attributed to his mother.

*The study at Dunmore House today: it was fitted out by either Hugh or Patrick Gillies as a dispensary and consulting room.*

# 2  Some Rites of Passage

THE COMPULSORY EDUCATION Act had been in force less than two years when, in 1874, Patrick Gillies was old enough to start school. The new legislation had little immediate effect upon the slate villages which were already served by a relatively efficient education system. Soon after the formation of the Easdale Marble and Slate Quarrying Company in 1745, Breadalbane had provided schooling for the children of his quarry workers and others on his estates. Although by 1874 the parish school, which was at that time situated on the outskirts of the village of Balvicar, had fallen into disrepair there were a number of small, privately run schools in the district – on the islands of Luing, Belnahua and Easdale, at Caolas and at Clachan – which were operating successfully. It is almost certain that the infant Patrick began his school career in the house of one of the ladies of Caolas who provided basic education for a few pupils in her own front parlour.

One of the provisions of the 1873 Education Act was the formation of a school board to oversee the provision of education within each parish. In the parish of Kilbrandon and Kilchattan, by virtue of their position in the community, this body included among its number Doctor Hugh Gillies and Angus Whyte, the manager of the Easdale quarries. The first task of the new board was to raise money sufficient to build schools and accommodation for a schoolmaster in each of the major villages in the parish.

The Education Department (Scotland), which was based at Westminster, gave a substantial grant towards the cost of these buildings but the remainder of the money, which had to come from the local community, was provided by the Easdale Quarrying Company augmented by private subscription. The land was donated by Breadalbane and the schools were constructed to a standard pattern designed by Breadalbane's own architect and used for similar buildings throughout his estates.

Four schools were planned for. One of these was at Clachan (Ardencaple School, not far from the Clachan Bridge), two others were to be built in the villages of Cullipool and Toberonochy on Luing, and the fourth at Easdale. Three of the schools were completed and handed over to their schoolmasters in the year 1877. At Cullipool, where the parish school had been established in a fairly substantial building belonging to the quarrying company and was running very efficiently, the board decided to delay expenditure on any new construction until the three other schools in the parish were considered to be running satisfactorily. It was a pattern all too familiar in local government enterprise. Building of the fourth school, at Cullipool, was delayed for so long it never materialised!

Patrick was eight years old when, together with his younger brother Hugh and his sister Janet, he became one of the first pupils at the new Easdale Public School, under its headmaster, Mr Stewart. It is unlikely that John Gillies ever attended the new school. Although the Education Act had provided for pupils to remain in school until the age of thirteen years, the old custom of releasing children at eleven to become apprenticed to a trade still held sway. John would have been eleven when the new school was opened and his parents saw nothing wrong in allowing him to forgo the remainder of his schooling in order to take his place amongst the farm workers where he might best learn his trade. John's passion was farming and he could not wait to get started.

For the first few years John was content to share the work of Dunmore Farm with his mother and her small band of labourers. The promise of riches and adventure overseas was however a tremendous lure for young men of the time and John spent his leisure hours planning with his friends how they would go abroad at the very first opportunity. Realising that the lad would never rest until he had got the wander bug out of his system, Jessie and Hugh agreed that he should go abroad, but not until he had reached the age of seventeen. It was with a heavy heart that, six years later, Jessie was to wave her first-born off on his travels. Her strategy paid off, however, for John eventually returned to Easdale to manage Dunmore for his mother until her death in 1907.

Easdale School and school-house, Ellenabeich. From as early as 1863, when Hugh Gillies came to Easdale, quarry workers' children were obliged to attend school from age 5 until 11. When Patrick was a pupil, from 1874 onwards, the normal leaving age was 13, although boys as young as 11 still worked in the quarries, attending night school until they were 13. Until year-round attendance became compulsory under the Education (Scotland) Act of 1873, agricultural workers' children attended school only in the winter months. During the growing season they were expected to work on the land.

All the children studied Religious Knowledge, Reading Writing and Arithmetic, the parents paying a small sum of money once a term which was supplemented by the Quarry Company. Paupers' children attended school free of charge. For an additional payment (2s 6d or 12p) another subject might be added. History, Geography, Latin, Greek, German and French, Science and Navigation were all on offer as part of the curriculum when Patrick attended the school.

There were no school meals provided. A child's 'piece' probably consisted of a slice of bread and dripping or other 'scrape'. In a talk given to the children at Ardencaple School in 1901, the Inspector of the Poor described, while reminiscing about his own school days c.1850, how every child was expected to carry a coal to school to add to the classroom fire. Those who came without sat farthest from the stove.

*Patrick's university certificates indicate the esteem in which he was held by his tutors. The award of a degree was based upon these termly assessments, together with the final* viva voce *and written examinations.*

Patrick and his brother Hugh appear to have been outstanding scholars taking, in addition to the general curriculum of reading, writing, arithmetic and religious knowledge, Latin, Greek, French and German. Geography and history were included with these extra subjects, all of which were paid for at two shillings and sixpence per subject, per term, around thirty to forty pounds by today's standards. This was a considerable sum of money by the standards of the day and, since both boys remained at school until they were fourteen, a severe drain upon the family's resources. It is unlikely that their sister Janet studied to this extent. When she left school at the age of thirteen she became companion and housekeeper to a cousin of her mother. She remained unmarried and when Hugh eventually established himself and his family at New Abbey in Kirkcudbrightshire she went to join them. If Janet was no academic genius she does appear to have inherited from her mother a deal of good sense and practical ability for the family appears to have relied heavily upon her in future years, particularly at times of stress.

If anything, Hugh junior was marginally the brighter of Dr Gillies' sons but whereas Patrick was determined upon a medical career from the start as a boy his younger brother dreamt only of going to sea. Despite his early rejection of a career in any one of the three major professions, law, medicine or the church, Hugh studied the classics. He also took classes in navigation, however, and this gave him a considerable advantage when, at the age of seventeen, he joined the *Royal George* as an apprentice and set sail for the Antipodes.

Both Patrick and Hugh spent much of their leisure time with the village lads and, since the sea was a major factor in everyone's lives, they learned to handle the small craft which were used to travel between the islands. Because his medical practice was largely scattered amongst the small isles, Dr Gillies kept a boat on the foreshore below Dunmore House, using it to attend patients in an emergency as well as for routine visits to the quarry villages on Luing and Belnahua. Some Sundays, when the tide was right and the weather fine, the family would join a small fleet of vessels from Easdale and sail to Cuan to attend services at Kilbrandon Church. Between the islands of Seil and Luing there is a strong tidal race which makes it difficult to navigate unless the tide is in one's favour. It is said that the minister timed his sermons to coincide with the changes of the tide so that his parishioners could enjoy the benefit of an easy passage home!

These and other such family outings by sea appear to have been a regular occurrence and were much enjoyed by everyone, but the business of the medical practice had a much more serious, even dangerous side. While it was not common in the nineteenth century for working-class people to summon the doctor for every ill which beset them, nevertheless there were times when the doctor would be summoned no matter what the time of day or night or the severity of the weather.

On one such occasion in November of 1879 Dr Gillies was called to the bedside of a patient on the island of Luing. The patient, an elderly quarrier, had suffered a mild stroke some weeks previously forcing him to give up his work. Feeling recovered and anxious to earn money for his family, the fellow had returned to the quarries against the doctor's advice and was now stricken far more severely, seeming to be at death's door.

It was a miserable afternoon. The islands, which had been shrouded in mist all day, suddenly appeared sharply outlined against a grey sky, and as the rising wind veered towards the north-west, the clouds lifted and moved away southwards giving a clear indication that there would be a storm before nightfall. Eliza Bett and her husband were visiting Dunmore at the time and, as Eliza was to point out later, she and Jessie tried their best to dissuade the doctor from answering his patient's call. Hugh had been suffering for some days from a mild bout of influenza and should by rights have taken to his bed himself. He was certainly in no fit condition to be out and about in stormy weather. It was not in the doctor's nature however to ignore a call from one of his patients so, knowing full well that there was little he could do to save the man, he set out with one of the farm labourers to sail to Toberonochy.

By the time the doctor's small sailing craft drew alongside the quay in the sheltered harbour on Luing it was already raining hard and blowing a gale. While his man remained to secure the boat, Hugh trudged through the village the half mile to his patient's cottage where he found the old quarrier close to death. Still in his wet clothes, Hugh worked ceaselessly throughout the night in order to ease his patient through his final hours. After a long travail, the patient eventually died, and towards dawn the doctor set out on his homeward journey. It was fortunate that he had a companion with him because without a second pair of hands at the oars, Hugh would never have reached home. Together the two men manoeuvred their tiny craft into the teeth of the storm. Although the tide was in their favour, the wind was against them and they were obliged to reduce sail and row. The time taken for their journey was thus trebled. To keep the vessel under control in such conditions demanded the strength of both men and by the time they had secured the craft on the beach below Dunmore, they were exhausted.

Hugh managed to stagger to his door where he collapsed and was carried to his bed. His mild dose of influenza became a severe chill which quickly developed into pneumonia. Medical help was summoned from Oban but, without benefit of antibiotics, recovery was dependent solely upon the patient's general strength and nothing more. Despite the best efforts of his colleagues, Hugh Gillies remained on the sick list for some weeks and it became necessary to engage a locum doctor.

The young man who answered Jessie's call for assistance was an undergraduate medical student, Mr Connal Wilson. Wilson had been preparing himself for his final examinations in Edinburgh before sailing for Cape Town where he hoped to practice medicine. Despite his lack of experience, the young man settled quickly into his new role and was soon a familiar figure around the district. For many weeks he ran the medical practice, lodging in the doctor's house and becoming almost one of the family. In addition to his other duties, Connal Wilson attended Hugh and supervised his nursing. Dr Gillies remained an invalid for many months, making little sign of recovery until, in July 1880, his heart finally gave out. Connal Wilson was in attendance at the time of Hugh's death and remained with the family for some weeks afterwards until Jessie could make a more permanent arrangement about the medical practice. The tragic circumstances in which he had come to know the family created a bond between Connal Wilson and Jessie Gillies which was to last for many years to come.

Hugh's death at the age of forty-four had come as a great shock to everyone. The severity of the blow to his happy little family is unimaginable. John, the oldest of Jessie's six children was thirteen. The youngest, Lizzie, was only three. The Easdale community was overwhelmed by the tragedy and Jessie received a great many black-bordered letters of condolence, filled with pious platitudes it is true, but underlain by the sense of genuine grief at the loss of such an important figure to the parish. The church was filled to overflowing for the funeral and so great were the numbers crowded into the Kilbrandon cemetery on the edge of Balvicar village that many mourners had to stand in the field beyond the kirkyard wall. The impressive obelisk, raised by public subscription, bears witness to the esteem in which the doctor was held by the community.

With such a large family on both the Hunter and Gillies sides, Jessie never lacked advice. Within days she received from her sister Eliza Bett a letter expressing her family's great sorrow at the death of her brother-in-law. Eliza had been at Dunmore on the day Hugh returned home from his stormy adventure and had stayed on for some days during her brother-in-law's illness.

When I said goodbye to yourself and your dear husband I had no idea that such a sad change was at hand. I was told by Mr Bett that he felt sure the doctor would get strong again but I could not agree and that day when he left in the small boat convinced me of his great weakness and that quite upset me . . . I was talking to Mr Bett lately about your outstanding accounts that I feared they would not be paid readily and he thought you ought to give them all to McArthur in Oban to collect both, professional and for the milk. But you will know best the feelings of the people, whether they show sympathy for you and are willing to pay without being forced which would be very unpleasant for all . . . I have been looking out some cast-offs and should I find anything that would suit your boys perhaps you would not object to taking them . . . Now Jessie promise me you will not hesitate to write Mr Bett to consult him on business matters as he will be always ready to give his advice to aid you.

With love to yourself and the children I am your affectionate sister,

Eliza Bett

[ellipses original]

The assumption that Jessie was incapable of dealing with her husband's debtors herself may well have incensed her, for Jessie, unlike many married women of her day, was fully conversant with her husband's affairs and in all probability wrote out patient's accounts on his behalf as well as dealing with all matters relating to the farm. She might not have been all that pleased either to be offered so immediately cast-off clothing for the children. She could well have been outraged at the assumption that as a widow she now fell into the category of a charitable cause with which her sister might ease her social conscience!

Other members of the family were less suffocating. Her brother Alexander Hunter, who had emigrated to Canada some years earlier, waited until the following year to invite her to bring her family to Ontario:

Woodburn, Hamilton, Ontario 21.5.1881

[. . .] You are no doubt getting along pretty well and I trust you are, but if you could make up your mind to come across to this glorious country I feel that after the first year or so you would come to like it for the better. I should be glad to hear good news from you.

Yours very sincerely, A Scott Hunter.

Had Jessie taken this advice there would have been a very different outcome not only for the Gillies family but for all those whose lives were to be touched by Patrick in the years to come. Jessie was too strong a character, however, to allow herself to be diverted from her chosen course.

Whether or not she acted upon, or welcomed any of the advice she received it is hard to say for what became clear, at a very early stage, was the widow's determination to retain the family home, and in particular the farm, which she was quite capable of managing alone. She was adamant also that the future which her husband had mapped out for their children should be safeguarded. Although Hugh's appointment as medical officer to the quarries was in the hands of Breadalbane and would have to be passed on to some other doctor, the private practice, built up by her husband during his twenty years working in the district, was Jessie's to sell or retain as she saw fit. She chose to engage a series of locum doctors, young men unable to afford a practice of their own

*The obelisk erected in Kilbrandon cemetery to commemorate the life and work of Dr Hugh Gillies.*

but seeking to earn the wherewithal to do so. In this way she was able to hold on to the private part of the family business in hope that one of her sons might eventually take it over.

Jessie received letters of condolence from all around the country, from Hugh's professional associates as well as family and friends. It was clear that her husband had spread his good work far and wide and people were appreciative. When it came to managing her affairs and raising her very young and rather large family, however, she soon discovered that, financially at least, she was on her own. Plenty of pious utterances were forthcoming from such people as the Rev. Dr Graham of Campbeltown who, considering himself to be something of a patriarch in the Hunter circle, offered a six-page epistle extolling the virtues of humility, tolerance and clean living and suggesting guidance in the matter of the boys' (Patrick and Hugh) reading of the classics. While Jessie's sisters wrote kindly, they could make no financial contribution constrained as they were by their husbands' wishes in the matter. Jessie's second brother, Robert, who like Alexander had gone to America, wrote too but in a somewhat different vein. No doubt anticipating that his sister's husband, being a professional gentleman, would have left her pretty well off, he sent a letter pleading for money to help him out of a hole.

This was not the first time Robert wrote home for financial assistance, for another letter exists, addressed to his mother, in much the same terms. Whether Jessie responded to his advantage is not known although this is quite probable. In the early days of her widowhood she seemed determined to show herself of independent means and to stay out of debt.

When the children returned to school after the Christmas holiday they took with them the fees for the coming term. A letter from Mr Stewart, the schoolmaster, conveys the sympathy felt by many of Jessie's neighbours at this time:

Burnside Easdale, Wednesday Morning

My Dear Mrs Gillies,

Being out walking when your note with enclosures was left here last evening I had no time to answer it until now. I can assure you I am sorry to see that you have thought of sending me the boys' fees. These I cannot accept. I shall do my utmost for them, money is what I never have in my calculations when teaching them. I think I treat them as I would like my own to be treated in similar circumstances and to wish them better or to work harder for their success, I cannot.

I am sorry we cannot for a few weeks pay your account. I trust you remember that you were to retain the MacIntyre's fees for me. I shall call up in the evening and have a talk whenever school comes out. I enclose cash and account.

Yours faithfully,

Robert Stewart

This apparent magnanimity is however not quite all it seems. Mr Stewart was noted for being tight fisted when it came to any matters related to money and what he appears to be suggesting here is that Jessie allow him to pay off his own debt to the doctor's account in kind (i.e. teaching time) rather than cash! One must not overlook the reference to the MacIntyre's fees which Jessie is holding on his behalf. A rather odd inclusion in what otherwise appears to be a letter of condolence! At another time this same Mr Stewart was the defendant in a rather unsavoury court case brought against him by a pupil teacher from whom he had been swindling the fees rightly earned by her while teaching the children 'extra' subjects. Jessie did not much approve of Mr Stewart as will be seen in further correspondence in which his name appears. He was however important to her plans for Patrick and Hugh and he seems to have been an excellent schoolmaster, even if the grammar in this letter is a little suspect! Both boys were educated to matriculation standard in the village school and gained direct entry to their university courses.

The MacIntyres mentioned by Mr Stewart were the minister's family, close friends of the Gillieses for the short period of the Rev. MacIntyre's incumbency in the parish of Kilbrandon and Kilchattan. The family at the manse were a welcome intrusion into the lives of the young Gillieses, who generally lacked contact with other children of their own class.

Among the numerous MacIntyre children Mary Davinia was Patrick's contemporary, being just a few months older than he. Like Patrick she was an outstanding scholar, and as a consequence the doctor's son found his own bright star somewhat eclipsed in the classroom. For the two years that Mary sat alongside him at the head of the class they were constant and deadly rivals for the teacher's accolades. When she left Easdale Mary went to the College for Daughters of Ministers of the Church in Edinburgh, where she excelled particularly in French and German.

At the age of fourteen years and some months, Patrick left the village school having achieved high marks in all his subjects. Mr Stewart was unstinting in his praise, presenting the young man with a glowing testimonial:

27th October 1883 Easdale Public School.

I hereby certify that the bearer Mr Patrick Gillies has attended this school since his childhood; that his range of studies was extensive embracing Latin, Greek, French, German, mathematics, chemistry as well as the ordinary branches; that his excellent talents and great perseverance enabled him to occupy a very prominent position in all his classes; that his conduct has been uniformly highly exemplary and that he is deservedly held in very great respect by all the teachers who wish him every success.

Robert Stewart, Headmaster

On leaving school, Patrick became apprenticed to the Oban pharmacist Mr Robertson. This was at the time an accepted means of preparing for his future medical studies. The journey from Easdale to Oban by the horse bus, took two-and-a-half hours. It was therefore necessary for Patrick to take lodgings in Oban, a situation which must have made quite a dent in his meagre earnings. Family legend has it that Patrick and Hugh, who also worked in the pharmacy for a year or two, walked home to Dunmore and back at weekends, starting out on Saturday evening when the shop closed and returning very early on Monday morning before opening time. Today the distance by road is sixteen miles but it may well have been possible almost to half this distance by taking a ferry across the mouth of Loch Feochan and travelling across country instead of by the road.

Patrick spent four years as an apprentice to Mr A. Robertson, before he entered Edinburgh University as a medical student in his eighteenth year. The full term for an apprenticeship was five years which makes the concession given an unusual one, almost certainly due to Hugh Gillies' standing within the local medical fraternity.

Mr A Robertson of Ino.Hunter            Oban, April 18th 1884
Family and Dispensing Chemist
and Aerated Water Manufacturer
Oban

To Mrs J Gillies
Dunmore house, Easdale

Madam,

I regret that I missed seeing you on Wednesday but was glad to hear you had secured such comfortable lodgings for Patrick. I would like him to start on Wednesday or Monday 27th if possible for I am getting pretty busy. I have been thinking over the wages question. My apprentice, Nicholson, receives £15; £15; £18; £20 and £22 as per the enclosed indenture, but his receiving £15 for the first and second years is exceptional and arose through his being originally engaged as message lad at 5/- per week and when I agreed to take him as an apprentice I did not think it advisable to lower his wages to £10 a year which is the regular amount. In the south it is much lower. Considering that your son is to serve four years, I will thus lose him during the year he would be of greatest service hence I would propose to regulate his salary thus: £10; £15; £18; £22. I will be glad to have your opinion.

Yours faithfully,

A Robertson

Jessie must have felt the wages offered were, under the circumstances, acceptable. The sum of £10 equates approximately to £1,500 today. At a time when it was more normal for an apprentice to pay a fee for the privilege of learning at his master's elbow, this was very generous. Had Hugh lived his son would undoubtedly have been signed up as his own apprentice and this experience in the pharmacy was without doubt the next best thing. There is a lot to be said for exposing students to the practical applications of their studies at an early stage. Today's work-sampling schemes of a few weeks during the final years at school are a poor substitute for the quality of experience gained by the Gillies boys in the Oban Pharmacy. Mr Robertson evidently found Patrick's work satisfactory because he provided a glowing testimonial when his apprentice presented himself at Edinburgh University for matriculation in 1887. Unconfirmed family tradition has it that Patrick, having completed the first two years of his course of study at the top of his class, was awarded the Ettles Scholarship for the most outstanding final year undergraduate. This would certainly have helped considerably in financing his last year at university. At that time, as well as receiving a diploma on the strength of written examinations and a *viva voce*, students were presented with a written testimonial from each of their professors at the end of every session. Patrick's final set of testimonials was outstanding in the uniformity of praise for his appreciation, application and practical performance in all subjects. Had he wished, he could have attained a very good post in a hospital and might well have risen to great heights as a surgeon. Against the advice of his mentors however, included amongst whom was no less a person than Joseph Lister himself, Patrick opted for his father's old practice at Easdale. There is little doubt that he felt an obligation to fulfil his mother's desire that one of her boys should carry on where their father had left off. She had, after all, made great sacrifices in order to send him to university.

Towards the end of his course of study Patrick wrote to his mother from his digs in Edinburgh, and while expressing the usual student doubts about the

A horse bus beside the Volunteer's Drill Hall at Ellenabeich. The horse bus was a great innovation in the Slate Islands in the latter part of the nineteenth century. According to Patrick Gillies the journey from Ellenabeich to Oban took two-and-a-half hours and passengers were expected to get out and walk up the steepest hills to rest the horses. The return fare to Oban was about 2s 6d or 12p, a sum which was generally beyond the means of many of the villagers! Prior to the introduction of the horse bus, islanders

travelled from village to village on foot or horseback, or took a lift on a farm cart. For greater distances, the steamer was the answer. From the 1830s until the 1930s, islanders who could afford the fare travelled to Oban, Fort William and even Inverness and Glasgow by steamer. The horse bus was succeeded in 1930 by a motorised charabanc which was housed at Caolas.

forthcoming examinations he cannot resist telling his mother about a rather typical student exploit:

16 Panmure Place
Edinburgh,

Dear Mother,

You will be thinking I am dead but I'm too busy to write even a letter home. I studied for twelve hours yesterday went to bed at 3.0 am. and got up again at 8.0 o'clock. I cannot tell whether I'll get through this or not still I have always a chance. Morrison has chucked the whole thing up till next April. His mother died last week and he had to go home and that spoiled his chances.

Its beastly weather here. Raining every day. Is Gordon [the locum running the Easdale practice] in Balachuan yet? Have you had a visit from him?

Is your house let? What are you asking this time? I hope it won't be a Glasgow beggar that gets it this time.

How is the world getting on about Easdale? I hear far more news about it from the Oban Times and other fellows than I do from home. Is Cameron ever coming over? I was visiting McLeod on Saturday last. I had tea and supper with him. He's about the jolliest fellow to spend an evening with of anyone I know. He kept me laughing from 6.0 o'clock to half past ten! What lies he does tell. He was advising me to go in for football next winter if I mean to pass my final in July next. I got my chanter from Fletcher yesterday [it seems that all the Gillies boys played the bagpipes]. McRae and I were up at McPhail's last Sunday but he was out. McRae by this time was hungry so went to McPhail's cupboard and got out half a loaf and demolished it along with a pot of marmalade which was three quarters full (He's an awfa' man for jam!) We then left. When we were on our way down Forrest Road (McPhail's digs are in Forrest Road) who should we meet but McPhail. 'Hallo you fellows where have you been?' asks McPhail. 'We've just had tea in a friend's digs,' says McRae. 'Well come up and have another supper, anyway,' says McPhail. McRae said we were too full and off we went. McPhail when he got home noticed the absence of marmalade and had a thundering row with his landlady but later he found out who did it and now I take a wide berth when I see him!

Hoping you are all well. Your affectionate son,

Patrick H Gillies

Jessie welcomed Patrick home with open arms. Once he had returned to Easdale, it became very apparent that in spite of his being only the second son, Jessie regarded him as the head of the family and was happy to offload on to him much of the burden she had borne alone since her husband's death. We have no idea what John's reactions were to the elevated position now held by his younger brother. Patrick's close association with his father from his early childhood, added to the general assumption that he would be the doctor's natural successor, had instilled in the newly qualified doctor an acute sense of his responsibilities towards all those nearest and dearest to him. His mother's brave struggle to survive financially had made Patrick very aware of the need to keep a tight rein upon expenditure and this may well have contributed to the impression he gave as he grew older, of being a miserly, rather nick-picking personality where finances were concerned. Even when he had been elevated to the most senior medical office in the county, Patrick still counted the pennies. There is, however, plenty of evidence of his generosity with money. He never failed to attend the poorest patient even when he knew there would be no remuneration and he personally financed his sister's schooling at a time when he himself was already burdened with a wife and growing family. It is a fact however that he pursued, relentlessly, every halfpenny owed to him by the quarry masters and the local authority!

Patrick's brother Hugh also spent three years at Robertson's pharmacy in Oban, possibly only as a message boy for he was merely killing time before embarking upon his naval career. He joined his ship, the sailing barque *Royal George*, as a midshipman on 16 Jan 1888. Within two days she sailed for Australia carrying a mixed cargo from Middlesborough to Adelaide. Five weeks later Jessie was writing to Hugh from her much depleted household at Dunmore. John was home from Canada for a spell but Patrick was away in Edinburgh and her daughter Jessie, now fifteen, was helping to take care of the children of a relative in Acharer. Only the two younger children were still at school.

Jessie and Hugh exchanged correspondence during his travels which indicated that life continued much as usual in Easdale while Hugh's accounts of life at sea reveal an environment which must have been quite alien to the young fellow brought up in the bosom of a close-knit, loving family. The overwhelming theme of Jessie's correspondence was her son's health and her concern that he should not get into bad company or take to drink. One may imagine that with such a limited experience of the world outside her own home and her life at Easdale, Jessie could base her knowledge of the world, and seafarers in particular, only upon her encounters with those seamen who came to Easdale to collect slate. Although her older son, John, had related his adventures overseas, these were connected more with the land and farming, and farmers were something Jessie could understand. Her letter to the captain of the *Royal George* requesting that gentleman to provide Hugh with small amounts of money should he need it and to take care of his spiritual as well as his physical well-being must have caused the young man no little embarrassment.

Hugh's voyage to Australia took more than four months, and it was not until he reached Port Pirie, near Adelaide in South Australia that he was able to correspond with his mother. His letters include accounts of severe weather in the Atlantic, a protracted period becalmed off the coast of Africa and the death of a shipmate, with a graphic description of his burial at sea. By the time the ship reached its destination it had become clear to the master and his senior officers that Hugh Gillies' eyesight was defective and that his chances of ever becoming a navigating officer were nil. For Hugh, whose childhood dream of a life at sea had been thus thwarted, it was a devastating blow softened only by the fact that he had found life on board rather harder than he had anticipated. Maybe his poor eyesight proved a satisfactory get-out for him by which he might leave the service without losing face. He certainly seems cheerful enough in his letter from Port Pirie of 23 June 1888, in which he declares, 'One of our apprentices, Garnett by name, has run away and out of fifteen hands there are only eight remaining. I do not intend to go until we reach home. Then, Goodbye *Royal George*!' Hugh's 'Goodbye, *Royal George*' seems to indicate an eagerness to be out of the navy as soon as possible; however, still preserving the fiction that he would have preferred to have remained at sea, he added as a postscript, 'Mother darling please believe me when I say that, despite all, I could stick this life if it wasn't for my eyesight.'

The *Royal George* became becalmed on her return passage through the doldrums. She was so long overdue that, in the belief the ship had foundered, the Lutine Bell was struck at Lloyds of London to indicate to stock holders that she was lost. Jessie was to spend several harrowing weeks before she received confirmation of Hugh's safe arrival in Scotland.

On his return home Hugh wasted no time in signing on for a series of courses in anatomy, materia medica, medicine and surgery at the Andersonian University of Glasgow, his father's alma mater. His 'gap year', as we would call it today, appears in no way to have inhibited his academic studies. Hugh successfully completed courses in both surgery and medicine, emulating his brother in achieving the double qualification of Licentiateships of the Royal College of Surgeons, Edinburgh and of both faculties, of Physicians and Surgeons, of Glasgow University in 1894. Awarded a number of honours and medals at each stage of the course, he completed his training as a dresser in the Glasgow Royal Infirmary. During Patrick's absence while taking a course for a BSc degree in Public Health, Hugh looked after the Easdale practice. Following the death of his mother a year later, he was able to use her not inconsiderable legacy to purchase a medical practice in New Abbey, Kirkcudbrightshire. He remained there for the rest of his life.

Patrick felt he had a particular obligation to protect the interests of his youngest siblings, Thomas and Eliza. At the time of his father's death, Tom was six and Eliza only three. Eliza in particular had scarcely known what it was to have a father. As he grew older, Patrick was the one to assume this role. Tom, like his brother John, was no scholar and was only too happy to leave school and to work on the farm.

With Eliza, Hugh's 'Little Doe', Patrick had no trouble at all. Eliza was a bright, pretty child who did very well at school and was liked by everyone. Patrick paid for her education at a private school in Edinburgh from where she went on to become a teacher. Having spent some years in this profession she finally met and married a Captain Beveridge and moved away to England. Three years after her wedding in October 1914, she was widowed at the age of forty when her husband was reported missing in France, presumed killed in action.

Undoubtedly, amongst his own generation, however, Patrick's favourite was his sister Jessie. When, in a tragic road accident, she died at the age of thirty-eight, Patrick described this generous-hearted, uncomplaining woman who had spent her life taking care of the needs of others as 'the best of them all!'

# 3 Early Days in the Easdale Practice

PATRICK GILLIES HAVING achieved honours in many subjects, left university with a double first-class honours degree in medicine and surgery and a fistful of excellent recommendations from his tutors, in particular from Professor Chieve for whom he acted as dresser during his final year. As we have already seen, with any number of good hospital posts open to him he chose instead to fulfil his boyhood dream of stepping into his father's shoes and he returned to Easdale in 1890.

The way was made easy for him in that the doctor presently holding the post of quarry medical officer, Dr MacDonald, was about to resign his position and Breadalbane had made it abundantly clear to all concerned that he wanted the newly qualified young Dr Gillies to succeed him. Patrick's work as medical officer to the slate quarrying company brought him into contact with both workers and their families but it was to accidents in the quarries that he was summoned most often.

> What might have proved a very serious accident occurred at the Balvicar Quarry the other day. A young man named MacDougall son of the foreman of the quarry, accidentally fell into the quarry which has a depth of about forty foot. He was for sometime thereafter unconscious but by the ready and skilful treatment at the hands of Dr Gillies, MacDougall, we are pleased to learn, is progressing satisfactorily.
>
> *Oban Times*, 26 May 1900

In May 1901 the *Oban Times* reported a serious blasting accident which took place at the Glenalbyn Slate Works at Clachan. This was one of the smaller

The *Chevalier* was one of a number of steamers serving the west coast route between Crinan and Fort William when Patrick lived and worked at Easdale. She called twice a day at Easdale pier, Ellenabeich, and at Blackmill Bay on Luing: once on the southbound leg of her journey, arriving at Easdale about noon and also when northbound at approximately three o'clock. Passengers joined the Linnet for the trip along the Crinan Canal to Ardrishaig and then transferred to one of the Clyde steamers for the remainder of the voyage to Glasgow. It was possible to reach London by boat and train in 24 hours.

enterprises undertaken by individuals as a small consortium who, for one reason or another, were currently not employed in the main quarries. They would
produce slates in the hope of selling them either to the manager of the quarrying company or to meet some local demand. Such operations were, of course,
without supervision from a proper engineer.

> While Mr Charles Buchanan was confining a charge of powder in a boring the charge
> suddenly exploded injuring him severely about the face and hands. Dr Gillies found it
> necessary to amputate the left hand above the wrist. It [the arm] is also fractured above
> the elbow. He is badly burnt about the face. Four men who were working beneath
> the stage when the blast occurred escaped miraculously with only scratches. Foul air
> is supposed to be the cause of the premature explosion as all the tools used conform
> with what is laid down in mining operations, copper rather than steel being employed
> when using gunpowder.

One cannot help being suspicious of the reporting of this incident. Foul air is
the cause of explosions in enclosed spaces such as mines, where men are often
working in a confined space. Here, however, the man was boring into rock in
the open air. It is much more likely that the tool used for packing the explosive
was steel rather than copper which, being a much more expensive commodity,
would probably not have been available to this little group of entrepreneurs!
A spark from a steel tool might well have set off the gunpowder, particularly if
powder had been placed carelessly, too close to the drilling operation. It would
seem that those responsible for the tragedy were trying to blame an Act of God
for their own lack of care thereby avoiding any claim for compensation!

Despite medical successes which had begun to build his reputation as a surgeon, it was not long before Patrick realised that he lacked the experience
required to fulfil his duties adequately. Remembering his tutor's advice – 'if you
are determined to go into private practice, for God's sake get some experience
in a hospital first!' – he appointed a locum to fulfil his duties in the Easdale
Practice and in 1891 took the post of house surgeon at the Sheffield Public
Hospital. Here he encountered all manner of patients, from the poorest street
vagabonds to the wealthiest merchants, and almost every kind of accident and
disease the human frame might endure. Following a period of some months at
the Sheffield, he spent a few months as house physician in an asylum for the
insane at Carlisle. While the first of these two appointments was to stand him in
good stead during his time at Easdale, the second proved of inestimable value
when, towards the end of the Great War in 1918, he found himself having to
assess cases of 'shellshock' for pensions benefit. This condition was at the time

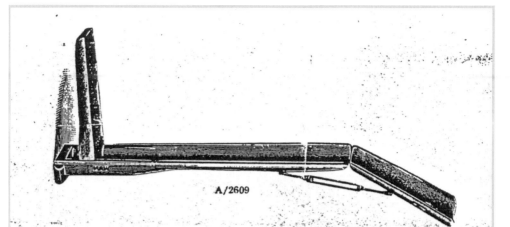

A/2609

Leg and Thigh Splints—Contd.--

'2609 Back Leg and Thigh Splint, hinged at knee, with adjustable foot pie
3 sizes.

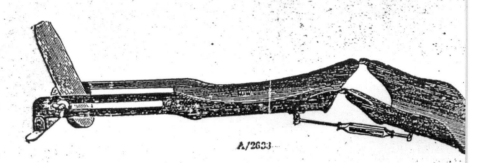

A/2633

A/2633 McIntyre's, japanned iron, with screw extension, 3 sizes.

Diagram of fracture apparatus taken from a catalogue of medical appliances of c.1890. Patrick was often called upon to attend to fractured limbs. A set of leg splints similar to those in the diagram was discovered on Easdale Island and is presently on display in the Easdale Island Museum. Without ready access to a hospital, emergency surgery was often carried out on the kitchen table and it is a tribute to Patrick's appreciation of the importance of aseptic methods that there are no recorded incidences of any of his patients dying from septicaemia following surgery. By the time Patrick took up his practice at Easdale ether was commonly in use during surgical procedures of this kind although he found that no such luxury was available on the battlefield in the South African war.

treated with some derision by the higher echelons of the armed forces. Only through the persistence of medical men such as Patrick Gillies was it eventually recognised as a genuine war-induced disability worthy of a disability pension.

During Patrick's two-year absence the medical contracts for both the Easdale and Luing quarries had been allocated to a Dr Gordon and there was some concern that Patrick's income might be seriously depleted when he returned to the Easdale practice in 1892. Jessie was able to reassure him when she wrote prior to his return from Carlisle. Despite her apparent confidence that Patrick would be made very welcome in the parish, Jessie seems to have been having second thoughts about the wisdom of his returning to Easdale at all. In this letter she expresses some concern that he might do better in his profession were he to apply for posts elsewhere.

Dunmore House
11th February 1892

My dear Pat,

I intended writing you this forenoon but could not find time as Jessie is in Luing preparing the class for the concert on Friday – tomorrow.

You would notice in the [Oban] Times what is going on here about the School Board etc. There was a fearful storm at the Monday meeting. I think Elsie has written you of the particulars. Should they appear in the Times tomorrow I will send them on to you. This is at present a most horrible place. What a blessed thing we can manage to steer clear. When the baker said at the meeting that they would hand in the note of their expenses for the board to pay, Hall said 'Faith Hugh, I'm no so sure of that.' Making them believe they would have to pay themselves. [Dr] Gordon said he had not a sue and couldn't pay them.

With reference to Gordon, we're led to believe that he has got his notice to quit but still cannot say for the truth of it. But Mr Kemp, Luing, told Hugh McLean that the moment Gillies [no direct relation] gets Gordon cleared out, you should think of coming here. He will promise you Luing, that is so far good. I cannot advise you upon that point at all. No doubt the whole practice put in one would be very good but still, would you not rise higher in your profession and social sphere other than here?

There is another project which I have heard mentioned with your coming here that this house is again looked upon as the Doctor's House. To this we have no objection and think it could be divided and arranged that you could have the front part to yourself and keep your own servant girl and boy and at the end of our lease other arrangements could be made.

I thought Jack was quite finished with Vancouver but a post card today has given him another idea that he is almost sure of it. I enclose you the whole affair from first to last . . . Jack should like to go to America. What he thinks is this; his expenses are all paid. He will see America and the appointment may be a stepping stone to a better life. Let us hear what you think of it all through. Should he get this [job]? We would all be all the better of your guidance here. I am a little afraid of Lorn [leaving?] but we must do our best [Lorn appears to have been the shepherd engaged to cover John's work]. I think between all the letters it will be enough for you to get through.

Trusting you are well.

I am yours affectionately

J Gillies

*Easdale distillery with Ellenabeich in the middle distance c.1930. Easdale Island lies in the background.*

Returning to Dunmore House where, with the help of Breadalbane's agent, his mother had made the entire front section over for his use, Patrick at once took on his duties as medical officer to the parish. At this time his private patient list was a short one and the income from the Kilbrandon and Kilchattan parish small. He had not yet secured the post of medical officer to the Easdale Slate Quarrying Company although this was just a matter of time. In order to increase his income he also applied to the Parish Council of Kilninver and Kilmelfort to secure the post of medical officer there.

> In the appointment of a new medical officer it was resolved that the salary be fixed at ten pounds per annum, nine pounds of salary as medical officer and one pound as public vaccinator. Certificates in lunacy cases of removal – the fee to be one guinea as formerly and no extra allowance for hire. It was further resolved that the medical officer will be bound to hold two diets of vaccination in the year for children other than paupers: time to visit to be at the discretion of the Parish Council, the doctor being entitled to charge the parents the usual vaccination fee of two shillings and sixpence. The clerk is instructed to send the doctor appointed a copy of these regulations for his signature. The council next proceeded to the appointment of a Medical Officer.

A vote by ballot was taken. The result was as follows.
Dr Gillies 4 votes
Dr MacCalman 3 votes.
Dr Gillies was accordingly elected Medical Officer and Public Vaccinator.

Parish Council meeting minutes 22 Nov 1901

Patrick's earnings came from many similar sources. For the year 1905 they were £394 (approx. £60,000 today) and for 1906, £390. This was made up of fees from the various quarries – Easdale, Balvicar, Clachan and Port Mary on Luing – the parish councils of Kilninver and Kilbrandon, and various insurance arrangements with Friendly Societies.

Patrick quickly settled into a routine which took him regularly to the quarry villages on the islands of Seil, Luing, Easdale and Belnahua. In addition, those landowners, farmworkers and their families who had been cared for by various locums since his father's death now became his private patients.

During the twelve years since Hugh Gillies' death the deterioration in the conditions of the quarrymen had become more marked and Patrick was to report an increasing number of cases of enteric (typhoid) fever in the years 1893 to 1897. The Local Government Act of 1883 had placed certain statutory duties upon medical practitioners to report such cases to the county medical officer for health and to the Sanitary Department. As Patrick moved about the parish he became aware of increasing problems concerning waste disposal which gave cause for alarm. Public drainage facilities in the villages were now stretched to the limit by the increasing number of occupants. Systems for the collection and disposal of both human and household waste were at best inadequate but more usually non-existent. After a few tentative approaches to the Local Authority for some improvement, Patrick found himself up against a brick wall because of his own lack of knowledge of modern sanitation engineering. When the county's sanitation engineers gave him their highly technical explanations for doing little or nothing in the way of improvements he was in no position to refute their claims and invariably lost his arguments.

On a brief visit to the village of Ellenabeich after an unusually dry spell of weather, the borough engineer had noted the open drain serving the main street and declared it an eyesore. Without further consultation with the villagers he ordered it covered. The drain had very little fall from the end of the street to its outlet into a disused quarry but while it remained open to the skies

Front Street, Ellenabeich, showing one row of quarry workers' cottages. The houses were owned by the Quarry Company who deducted the rents from each 'pay', which usually took place twice a year. Rents varied but an average household would have paid about three shillings (15p) per half year. This represented approximately 1% of annual earnings, but the houses were tied to the job meaning that when a man moved on to work in another quarry, retired or took alternative employment he was obliged to vacate his house. On the left of the road are gardens from which families could supplement meagre food supplies with their own produce, usually potatoes, turnips and green vegetables. The slate quarriers' cottages, often housing 6 to 8 people, were built to the same plan on all the islands. Two rooms, each some 13 feet square, were separated by a narrow hall to the front. Behind this was a larder press, and a box bed accessed from the kitchen side. The stone walls were up to a metre thick, the space between the outer and inner leaves being infilled with rubble. Roofs which in the late eighteenth century had been thatched with reed or heather were later replaced by slates deemed too small for export and provided free of charge by the Easdale Quarrying Company. Natural daylight was afforded by two small windows in each room and there were chimneys in the gable-end walls. The cottages were usually terraced, each having an outhouse and a small yard. Human and domestic waste was collected in a midden close to the sea and washed by the high tide. Water supply came from a standpipe at the end of the village street. Generally this would be sourced from a lochan high above the village except in the case of Easdale Island where a lead pipe fed water under the ocean from a reservoir on the Isle of Seil. In comparison with the houses of agricultural workers in the locality and those of miners and quarriers in other parts of Scotland these were exceptionally fine dwellings. With extensive improvements many of the houses are still occupied today.

*The post office was always the hub of village life. A postal service was introduced at Kilninver, 8 miles to the east, in the first quarter of the nineteenth century but by 1850 Easdale had its own postmark and post office, housed in the cottage which is now the Slate Islands Heritage Centre.*

the frequent rain showers were sufficient to move the waste along and ensure that the gulley was kept relatively clean. Once the engineer had had it closed over, however, the drain frequently became blocked, and foul water, backing up behind the blockage, ran out into the street and soaked into the foundations of the houses. In a report on the recurrent outbreaks of enteric fever in the village of Ellenabeich during the years 1888 to 1895 written in March 1896 Patrick made some interesting observations:

> The drain [at Ellenabeich] was constructed in 1888 and the next year, 1889, the first case of typhoid appeared. In 1890 there was a second. In 1892, three cases broke out. In 1894 there was one case and in 1895, three. In all there have been nine cases of typhoid occurring in six infected houses. All these houses lie on the NE side of Main Street. Not one house has been affected on the south side of the street [. . .] The south row of houses is built upon solid rock [the original rim of the old quarry] the north row on slate rubbish [infill] The drain lies midway between. Also, in the rubbish the ground slopes from south to north [indicating that any foul water must flow

towards the infected houses]. During hot periods of the year such as we experienced in September 1895, when the last cases occurred, the prevailing wind is S.S.W. Should any infection arise from the drain the moist foggy atmosphere should be a capital carrier. The prevailing wind blows fog and germs through the doors and windows which the inhabitants have left wide open in the heat of the day.

In an attempt to qualify this theory, Patrick goes on to say that 'It may be that the infection is spread in the soil water which trickles through and from the rubbish below the houses but there has been no Typhoid in the Front Street, (also) built on slate quarry rubbish.'

Here Patrick reveals the confusion, then current, concerning the transmission of the disease. Although he had seen the typhoid bacillus for himself under the microscope he appears not to have identified it as an exclusively water-borne infection. It was still commonly believed several decades into the twentieth century that germs were carried in moist air and particularly at night.

Although the sources of diseases such as typhoid and cholera were not yet fully understood, Patrick was certain that there was a relationship between the outbreak each year, during August and September, of enteric fever and the covered drain in Ellenabeich village. The problem was to convince the borough engineer of the legitimacy of his claims. Until he had acquired the necessary knowledge of sanitary engineering to hold an informed discussion with the man, Patrick knew he would be wasting his time. All he could do was wage a continuous battle with the authorities to have the houses properly disinfected after every outbreak of fever and educate the people in the most up-to-date hygiene practices. The quarriers' cottages were small, often having several members of a family sleeping in one room. When one individual became sick with an infectious disease, no matter how carefully Patrick's hygiene rules were applied, it was impossible to prevent the infection from spreading. After two seasons of battling hopelessly against impossible odds, he began his crusade for the establishment of an isolation hospital for the parish.

While the Local Authority did little to improve sanitation in the district, the Easdale Quarrying Company, for its part, invested considerable sums of money in supplying fresh water to the quarry villages. The purpose for this apparent magnanimity was, however, more closely related to ensuring an adequate supply of fresh water for use in the production of steam to drive the machinery rather than improving the lot of the villagers themselves. Nevertheless, in his

1895 report to the county medical officer of health Patrick praises these inner-
vations made by private individuals, possibly in hopes of shaming the county
councillors into taking action themselves, for although the quarry villages now
benefited from a good supply of fresh clean water this was far from the case in
other parts of the parish.

The new Easdale water-supply system was constructed by damming a small
lochan above Ellenabeich village and laying a series of iron pipes from the reservoir thus created to a large concrete cistern which in turn supplied the village
standpipes and the quarries. There was still no running water in the individual
houses but a new lead pipe was laid across the sea bed of Easdale Sound to supply the village on Easdale Island and the quarries there. As Patrick commented
in his 1895 report:

> There is just about sufficient storage capacity for one day's water, that is giving the
> population at, at least, 500 and the consumption per head the moderate one of ten
> gallons [45.5 litres; today the allocation is approximately four times this amount].
> It must be remembered that water is used for manufacturing purposes as well as for
> cooking, ablution etc. … Lord Breadalbane provided pipes and plumbers, the men of
> the villages opened and closed the trenches, while the Company, I believe, shared part
> of the expenses of the work.

It seems that the other villages in the parish were less well served. At Toberonochy the villagers had petitioned the district committee for a water supply but
had encountered a hitch. At Balvicar it was again the lessees of the slate quarry
who had had to dig deep into their pockets to provide a good supply of fresh
water for the quarry workings and their own employees. There were others
in the village, however, for whom the company was not responsible and there
was a long-running battle with the district committee over payment for water
supplied to those who were not employees of the quarry company.

While the condition of housing in the quarry villages gave Patrick cause
for concern, that of other buildings within the parish was equally question-
able. As well as reporting upon the condition of the villages, Patrick found
himself responsible for investigating the condition of individual farm houses
and farm cottages:

> In connection with this part of my report I must again call attention to the suspicious
> nature of the wells supplying Stronghorn Farmhouse and the cottars houses
> at Kilbrandon. Also that there is no proper drain for the removal of waste water
> from the water tap at the corner of Edward McInnes's house in the Main Street of
> Ellenabeich.

These investigations, meticulously carried out by the doctor and reported upon in detail, were occasionally acted upon: 'I mentioned [in his report of July 1895] the fact that Ardencaple Farmhouse seemed to be insufficiently supplied with water. I am glad to say that a new plentiful supply for the house and barns has been proposed, a matter of no slight importance to a dairy farm.'

An outbreak of dysentery amongst the family of the local publican, Mr Weir, landlord of the Tigh an Truish Inn, was particularly alarming as it posed a threat to the customers of that establishment as well as to the household. In February 1894, Patrick reported to the medical officer of the district council in Oban:

Dunmore House                                                          20.02.1894
To Dr R McNeill, Oban

Dear Sir,

I have under treatment at present three cases of what appears to be sporadic dysentery. All the patients are children under four years of age. They live in the Tigh an Truish Inn. The symptoms are typical and I think it right to propose the cause as the condition of the WC and the drains which do not seem to be all that can be desired.

The WC although trapped has no proper flushing system and there is sometimes an offensive smell. There is not sufficient drainage for both soil and the surface water the former being always in a more or less stagnant condition.

I do not mean to imply that this is the cause of the trouble. Sporadic cases are usually supposed to be due to irritating ingestion, but if we attribute the trouble to these conditions it makes the suspicion of a graver variety of dysentery stronger and the case one worth notifying. If you think it worth while I shall be glad to examine the house thoroughly and report.

The response from Dr McNeill seems to have been positive because Patrick carried out a thorough inspection of the premises and reported back the following day that the inn was supplied from a large concrete tank situated on the slopes of the hill above the building. Although the tank collected water from a clear spring, it had been for some unknown reason placed ten yards from the spring. The burn carrying the water to the tank also received effluent from a nearby byre! Although the inn was equipped with an indoor WC, there was no automatic flushing sytem, only a continuous thin stream of water inadequate for removing solid water. Below the house the ground was boggy, suggesting that all this foul water was not getting away and was undoubtedly the cause of noxious smells complained of by the landlady. Nevertheless Patrick does not commit himself to the theory that it is the water which is the cause of the cases of dysentery: 'I am unable to state definitely the cause of the dysentery. The position of the well and its relation to the byres requires special mention.'

In 1894 the concept of bacteria being the cause of the more familiar diseases was still in its infancy and animalcules as small as a virus were unknown. Patrick, fresh from university and instilled with the traditional knowledge of old men frequently dogmatic in their views, would have hesitated to put forward to the county medical officer the ideas which progressive teachers such as Joseph Lister may have planted in his mind. When he got to know Dr McNeill better he found him to be receptive and supportive of most of Patrick's new-fangled notions.

In the course of his work Patrick was sometimes obliged to administer to patients outside the parish of Kilbrandon and Kilchattan but nevertheless within reasonable distance of the Easdale district. The Island of Belnahua was a short distance from Luing but lay in the parish of Jura, its population was a little over one hundred souls. Thirty quarry workers were employed in slate making and they, together with their families, occupied a small village in the south-east corner of the island. Because of the lack of cultivable land and any natural water supply the people were dependent upon Luing for their provisions, including drinking water, which had to be brought over in small open boats.

Anyone becoming helpless and infirm in these circumstances would be wholly reliant upon their neighbours. Patrick's plea to Jura's inspector of the poor in May 1894 for assistance for two such residents underlines in addition the problems experienced by poor folk who moved around the country during their working life instead of remaining in their place of origin. This must have been a fairly common problem in the parish since quarry workers were particularly itinerant, being moved, often by the same employer, to a different area where there was a demand for their services.

Sir I have been asked to bring to your attention, with a view to getting aid in money or nursing, the patients under mentioned:

1. Alexander Sanderson aged 74 years residing at present on Belnahua. A native of the parish of Bressay, Shetland, he left Bressay in 1856, married his present wife in 1863 and had no child with her. With his first wife he had a son Matthew Sanderson, Lighthouse Keeper on Fladda [a short distance from the island of Belnahua]. The son who is 33 years of age is married and has a family. His wages as a lighthouse keeper are small.

2. Mrs Bruce Sanderson, wife of Alexander, is aged 74 and belongs to the same parish as her husband. She resided in the parish of St Cuthbert's North Leith from 1863 to 1871. From 1871 to 1888 in Granton; 1889 to 1889 in Crail in Fife; 1889 to 1890 on the Isle of Mann and from 1891 to 1892 on Fladda with her son-in-law. For the last eighteen months she has resided on the island of Belnahua.

Belnahua is an island razed to sea level by centuries of quarrying. It offers little protection from the winds and must have been a harsh and desolate location, particularly in the winter months. Thirty quarriers and their families lived here and there was a village shop and a school. Owned during the 18th and early 19th centuries by the Stevenson brothers of Oban, Belnahua provided most of the slate for the roofs of that town. It was also the source of Viking gravestones and slates for many of the 12th-century castles of Northern Scotland. At the outbreak of war in 1914 the men downed tools and went off to fight. Shortly after, the women retired to more comfortable accommodation on Luing or on the mainland, never to return.

3.  The husband is almost completely paralysed. He cannot walk and his powers of utterance are almost gone. The wife is confined to bed and suffers from ovarian tumour. This is a cystic tumour of the left ovary of enormous size, three or four times the diameter of a man's head!
4.  Both are quite helpless and depend upon the charity of neighbours for both attendance and nursing. The son is, I believe, very good to them but he has his duties which confine him to the lighthouse for much of his time. I hope it will be possible for you to do something for these poor creatures. Probably they are chargeable to their native parish but as it is a case of necessity occurring in the parish of Jura I thought it my duty to report to you.

It was encounters with extreme poverty such as this which were to lead Patrick, who had become incensed by the callous attitude of the parish council towards the less fortunate amongst their neighbours, to write, under a pseudonym, to the *Oban Times* with 'A Plan for the Poor of Easdale' on 28 Jan 1894.

> The condition of affairs as at present existing in Easdale would be none the worse of the publicity afforded us by the public press. A little salutary criticism will do no harm but should be the means of doing much good if only in repressing the vainglorious and misplaced attempts of members of a certain clique which assumes that they 'have explained themselves' to the people. This assumption may be perfectly correct and truthful but until made aware of it through the columns of the Oban Times, I for one among Easdale quarriers was ignorant of the existence of such popularity.
>
> In other districts this is usually a season of peace and goodwill. The poor have their interests watched, the necessitous their wants supplied. The widow gets her barrel of meal replenished and her cruise of oil refilled. Her heart beats warmer and the wrinkled old face beams smilingly and contentedly when she feels that although decrepit and palsied and unable to earn her bread, the last days of her earthly pilgrimage are days if not of plenty at least of comfort and that the power which guides the storm and calms the elements considers also her needs and makes the rich benevolent and the neighbours charitable. In Easdale the picture of the poor is a different one. It is sad and inharmonious. Instead of the replenished grate and the cosy fire which the benevolence and endearing generosity of the powers that be can ill afford them, they have in compensation the visit of a sheriff's officer and a notice of eviction pending and summary ejectment. Five of the poor wretches thus threatened are over eighty years of age and these at least might be left unmolested in possession of the homes built by their forefathers for the few remaining years of their lives. It is said that the merciful shall obtain mercy. A day may perhaps come when even an old widow's prayers and good wishes shall prove a solace and of value.

With the introduction of the Local Government Act of 1883, the parish councils had been imbued with certain executive powers which made them responsible for handing out benefits to the poor and needy from money provided from the rates. Only those owning or leasing property yielding an income of at least ten pounds per annum had either a vote or the opportunity to stand for election to the parish council. No longer were the minister and the doctor invited to join the board by virtue of their standing in the parish as had been the case in Hugh Gillies's time. If Patrick wished to have a say in the important matters of poor relief handled by the parish councillors he would have to seek election himself. He became a candidate for election in the same year and receiving the support of all sides of the community he was elected. He remained a parish councillor until he left the district in 1912.

Among his less agreeable tasks as medical officer for the parish, Patrick was called upon to investigate cases of death in mysterious circumstances and to make a report to the procurator fiscal. On such a wild coast cases of people being swept overboard or of small ships capsizing and their crews drowning were common. Patrick was often called upon to visit a body lying on some remote shore having been swept in by the tide. Not only was this distasteful, the bodies on occasion having been drowned and immersed in sea water for long periods before being cast ashore, but Patrick had particular difficulty in recovering the fees for these, often onerous, additional duties.

> Report on a body found on the shore at Scarba February 6th. 1906
>
> I hereby certify on soul and conscience that acting upon the instruction of the police authority I proceeded on Tuesday 6th February 1906 to Bagh na Urrachann on the W coast of Scarba where the body of a man had been found on the evening of Sunday 4th February. On examination I found the lower portion of the body of a man in a very much decomposed condition the bones and ligaments with a very small amount of flesh being all that was left. A rib was found about 100yds to the south and the jacket. Still further to the north was also found a singlet. It is evident that it was some months on the shore and that the skull and chest had been battered on the rocks during the winter storms but further than identifying this portion of the skeleton as that of a middle aged man, no information can be added for the cause of death would have to be decided by other than medical evidence.
>
> P.H.Gillies, Easdale 7 Feb 1906

Other cases of suspicious death were less difficult for the doctor to assess, but no less harrowing, especially as in this case the victim was well known to Patrick.

> I hereby certify upon soul and conscience that on Sunday the 15th day of April 1906 at 8.00 pm. I was asked to visit James MacLean, Easdale, who was reported as being unconscious and in a dying condition. On examining the patient I found him to be suffering from symptoms which appeared to me to resemble those of poisoning but although suspicion pointed to that of ptomaine I was unable to certify the cause of death without a post mortem examination and dissection. The patient having died on the morning of the 16th April, on the 17th April, acting under the authority of the Procurator Fiscal, I made a post mortem examination of the stomach and its contents and can certify from the knowledge of the contents and the symptoms previous to death, that death was due to ptomaine poisoning from the taking of tinned food. [A not uncommon occurrence at the time.]
>
> PH Gillies. Ballachuan, Easdale 17 April 1906

There can be no greater tragedy in a family than the death of a child and when that death is due to a preventable accident it can leave a scar on the lives of the parents for ever. The cold facts as written in this report of 26 Dec 1906 bear no relationship to the agony felt by Patrick himself over this incident.

Report on the death by burning of Mary Campbell of Ellenabeich 13.12.1906.

I hereby certify on soul and conscience that I examined the body of Mary Campbell aged 8 years, at Ellenabeich on the 13th Dec 1906. I found extensive burns of the second degree extending over the front of the thighs, the abdomen and lower part of the chest and also upon the flexor aspects of the arms. The face was also somewhat involved. From the results of my examination and the previous history of the case I certify that death was due to shock following upon extensive burns of abdomen, thorax and the extremities.

Such accidents were not uncommon in these overcrowded conditions. It is possible that the child's nightgown, almost certainly made of highly flammable cotton material, had been blown into the flames of the open fire by a sudden draught from an opening door. In the ensuing panic it was some minutes before any meaningful attempt was made to smother the flames.

Some of Patrick's cases were unfortunate, not to say bizarre. The blacksmith, who, one may imagine, was a gentleman of ample proportions and prodigious appetite, was inclined to eat a breakfast appropriate to his size and strength. Having awoken late and with a full day's work awaiting him at the quarry forge, he bolted his food with disastrous consequences. Patrick reported to the procurator fiscal on 1 Nov 1895:

About half past nine o'clock on the morning of Wednesday 30th October 1895 I was called to see Duncan Clark, Blacksmith, Easdale who, I was told, had choked while eating his breakfast. I proceeded immediately to see the patient but on arrival at ten o'clock I found that life was extinct.

On examination of the body I found no marks of bruising or violence, the body was quite warm and rigor mortis had not set in. On passing my finger into the throat I found just behind the opening to the larynx a large mass of non-masticated food. I detached large portions with my finger and found it to be a piece of cooked beef. Most of the food was in the pharynx or the mouth but a small portion had passed into the oesophagus and had apparently been firmly grasped by the oesophageal muscles but the part lying in the pharynx, being too large to swallow, had occluded the laryngeal opening and had produced suffocation and a fatal result, death probably occurring in two or three minutes.

I hereby certify on soul and conscience that the cause of death of Duncan Clark Easdale, was choking followed by suffocation.

It was not only the diseases of poverty but also those encouraged by ignorance and indolence which most exercised Patrick during these early years. Accidents were inevitable in the quarries, where warning systems were often inadequate. By public lectures to quarrymen and villagers and by private instruction at the sick bed, Patrick did his best to overcome the ignorance which so often led to

*The Richie family, some of Patrick's private patients.*

unnecessary injury or death. Despite the willingness of his patients to listen to his instruction, however, Patrick's work would be to little avail unless he could change the mindset of his fellow members on the parish council and of the elected members of the Local Authority, who were in a position to carry out reforms. Determined to place himself in a position to beat the sanitation engineers at their own game, Patrick decided to enrol himself in a new course being set up at Glasgow University, for a BSc degree in public health engineering.

By this time Jessie was ailing and her daughter Janet had come home to nurse her. Jessie's father died early in 1896. In his will he left the Hunter family home to his eldest daughter, Barbara, who never having married had cared for her parents throughout their lives. Mr Hunter bequeathed his remaining assets, a number of farms and other properties which, when realised, amounted to a sizeable sum, to be divided between his other children. Unfortunately for Jessie she never had an opportunity to enjoy her considerable inheritance. Within months of her father's passing she too was dead.

Jessie's family gathered together for her funeral. John, already home from his travels abroad, agreed that he would, with Tom's help, carry on the family farm for the time being. Janet, called home to nurse her mother during her final days, stayed on at Dunmore to keep house for her brothers. Eliza was still at school while Hugh, having attained his MB, ChB degree at the Andersonian University of Glasgow had gone on to take his Diploma for Licentiateship of the Royal College of Surgeons (Edinburgh) in 1894. At the time of his mother's death he had completed two years as a houseman in one of the Edinburgh hospitals and was therefore available to take care of the Easdale practice in Patrick's absence.

Jessie had left her estate, which had been increased considerably by the money from her father, to be divided equally between her children. John's share proved sufficient for him to buy the lease on a farm of his own and Hugh could now consider purchasing a medical practice. Patrick's share was very welcome as he had committed more than he could afford in returning to university for a further year. Tom and Eliza, having no immediate plans for spending the money, stashed away their nest eggs for future use.

# 4 The Isolation Hospital at Cuan

PATRICK HAD SET out for Glasgow knowing his mother's days were numbered but confident that his brother Hugh would take good care of her and the practice in his absence. Perhaps in order to save money or maybe because he felt he deserved a short holiday, instead of taking the obvious route by steamer to Glasgow, he travelled on foot determined to walk all the way to the university. Extraordinary as this may seem today, before the introduction of the motor car it was quite common for people to cover long distances by this means. This was particularly true of the Highlander who often found it easier to walk straight across country, as the crow flies, than to ride by way of tortuous and poorly maintained roads.

Patrick's route would have been from the head of Loch Feochan via Glen Scammadale and over the Lynne of Lorn to Dalavich. From there he would have hired a ferry to take him across Loch Awe to Ardchonnel. His way then led by way of a pass between the two peaks of Cruach Mhor and Beinn Bhreac. From the highest section of the pass he could have looked back over the route by which he had come and viewed the entire twenty miles of Loch Awe, from the low-lying village of Ford in the south-west to Kilchurn Castle and behind it the mighty Cruachan, its peak shrouded always in cloud and standing gaunt against the northern skyline. The pass led him to Inverary where by taking the ferry across Loch Fyne to St Catherine's he could cut off the five miles around the head of the loch. Through Glen Crow, with its highest point at the Rest and Be Thankful, the going would have been easy because he was following

The introduction of the bicycle in the 1880s brought a new kind of freedom to the Slate Islands. Ladies as well as men now had greater mobility with a ready means of access to all the villages in the parish and social intercourse received a considerable boost. Dr Gillies had a bike which to the end of his days he spoke of as 'the machine'. Despite the extreme weight of these early bicycles with their fixed wheels, cyclists tackled the hills with relish, propping their feet on the mudguard when freewheeling downhill. When riding, skirts were worn a little shorter but hat sizes do not seem to have diminished. Hat pins were, however, much longer and more numerous.

General Wade's road, built during the last quarter of the eighteenth century to open up the country in hopes of suppressing the rebellious Highland clans. This part of Patrick's journey was a lonely one for there were scarcely any dwelling houses from St Catherine's to Arrochar at the head of Loch Long. At this point a narrow neck of land, barely two miles in width, divides Loch Long from Loch Lomond and the village of Tarbet. From there he would have proceeded to Dumbarton by way of Luss and Balloch, before entering Glasgow along the Great Western Road. The journey of between sixty and seventy miles might be accomplished, by a fit man stretching himself to the limit, in a single day. It is more likely however that Patrick broke his journey, most probably at Inveraray or Tarbet, where there were comfortable hotels to be found. In later years the doctor acquired a motorcycle and later still, a motorcar but he never lost his zest for walking and would trudge around his widespread practice on foot in preference to using either horse or carriage.

Patrick's studies at the university included sanitary engineering, hygiene and public health and the law appertaining to these. His wide-ranging course included a study of geology, chemistry and toxicology, construction surveying, mensuration and technical drawing. It goes without saying that he completed his BSc degree course with first-class honours, returning to the Slate Islands in July 1897 armed with the necessary tools to take up his battle with the Local Authority. He brought with him, however, a much greater prize than a roll of parchment tied with pink string, for his childhood friend and rival Mary Davinia MacIntyre had agreed to marry him.

While in Glasgow, Patrick had called frequently at the home of the Rev. MacIntyre, his father's old friend from Easdale. It was only a matter of time before one of these visits coincided with that of his old rival, the minister's daughter, Mary Davinia. Having excelled in most subjects during her school life and having left with a special prize in German language, Mary was now a teacher at the prestigious Dollar Academy for the Daughters of Gentlemen. In the intervening years each of the young people had progressed favourably along their separate career paths and there was no longer any of that old rivalry between them except perhaps in intellectual argument! Their renewed friendship quickly developed into something much warmer.

Like his father before him, Patrick had made an excellent choice of fiancée for not only was Mary Patrick's equal intellectually, but she had grown up in much

*Patick's wife, Mary Davinia Gillies at the age of 31.*

the same atmosphere of social conscience and unstinting service to others which was expected of a doctor's household. Throughout her childhood she had been used to strangers interrupting the family's pleasures, demanding the minister's support in their troubles. She was quite inured to her father being called away in the middle of a meal to attend a dying parishioner and she had spent her childhood trailing after her mother to all those sometimes irksome social events which a minister's wife was expected to attend. She would fall easily into such roles as chairman of the Women's Temperance League or secretary of the Women's Rural Institute. Mary MacIntyre was, in fact, an ideal candidate for the role of doctor's wife.

She was a good-looking woman. Like her fiancée, Mary was tall and fair with clear kind eyes, but with a certain firmness of expression that suggested, whether in the classroom or the nursery, she would brook no nonsense. Even after the birth of her four sons she retained her willowy figure and to her dying day remained an upright, forceful human being with a mind of her own.

In the months leading up to his marriage Patrick immersed himself in his medical and political duties. There followed a series of reports condemning the method of removing human waste from the villages of Easdale and expressing concerns about certain water supplies. However, quite apart from the need for a thorough overhaul of the sanitary arrangements generally, the first priority was the provision of a suitable place where sick patients could be isolated from the rest of the community.

In these days of fast travel by motor vehicle when, despite the narrow, tortuous route, the sixteen miles to Oban can be covered by ambulance or car in a little over thirty minutes, it is perhaps difficult to appreciate the need for a hospital which would serve only two thousand or so parishioners of Kilbrandon and Kilchattan. In 1894 the journey to Oban took two and a half hours by horse-drawn trap and necessitated the passengers dismounting from their carriage on the steepest gradients. It was out of the question to transport seriously ill patients to hospital in Oban. The same difficulty arose throughout Argyll and the provision of small local hospitals for isolated communities was not exceptional. At the time when Patrick first made his appeal for a hospital in 1894, the Local Authority had already acquired a number of prefabricated buildings, called Docker Huts, for the purpose. By 1895 one of these had been set aside for Easdale. When he actually saw the building proposed, however, Patrick was less than enchanted. In his 1895 report to the county medical officer of health Patrick explains what happened when a docker hut was delivered to Easdale:

In the month of November, The Sanitary Officials of the County had the Docker Hut hospital which had been for a considerable time in Oban, transferred to Easdale and erected on a site near the village of Ellenabeich. The site was selected as a temporary one and to allow of patients in a weak state after fever, being transferred to it while homes were being disinfected. But by the time the hospital was erected, the fever patients had practically recovered and the houses had been disinfected, so that it was unnecessary to remove them. Clothes etc. were taken to the hospital and there thoroughly cleaned by a woman sent from Oban for the purpose.

At the beginning of December when Scarlet fever broke out, the Local Sanitary Inspector received orders to repair the leakages which had developed meanwhile and install the two patients immediately, in the hospital. When the Inspector eventually arrived at the hospital for the purpose of arranging for the removal of patients from their home, he found the roof and window sashes leaking and large pools of rain water collecting on the floor. Until this was put right it was impossible to remove any patients to the hospital. Workmen were sent from Oban to repair the leakage, but by the time the hut was in proper order the patients were all well on the way to recovery.

[. . .] while the hut is an excellent device in an emergency and is very good if we have no better at our command, still no one would say that the hut has accommodation for a permanent and useful hospital. Its great use is for an emergency and here, in these out of the way places, it is available for sudden outbreaks of infection. We require much more than the hut however. A proper administration block is necessary with kitchen, nurse's room, bedroom etc. Now these additions, if to be carried out, will I trust, never be added to the hut in its present position. A much better site has been secured with one slight objection, that the water supply is not so abundant as it is at Ellenabeich. Still there is a very fair supply available and the site is more central in a quiet and secluded spot away from traffic and the curiosity of the public, yet accessible. The exposure is excellent and the shelter good. The soil is porous and easily drainable and lastly and of greatest importance in the case of fever which requires unremitting attention, it is close to the medical officer's house. This site is near Cuan Ferry at Ballachuan. If the District Committee behave as liberally to this parish as they have done in the case of Dalmally I am sure it would not be difficult to gather subscriptions of over one hundred pounds in the district, and with the total sum a permanent building of stone and lime could be erected, suitable for the wants of the locality better fitted to stand the storms of our coast, and more comfortable and inviting.

A house at Ballachuan a mile or so from North Cuan, appears to have been reserved by Breadalbane for the use of the various doctors appointed to the quarry villages during the nineteenth century. Apart from locums, only the Gillies doctors practiced at Dunmore House. When Patrick married, he too removed to Ballachuan House, a mile or so along the road from the old church. Patrick's fears that the authority might decide to extend the existing hut in its present position were quickly assuaged. During one of the fiercest of gales that winter, the hut blew away, pieces of it being strewn along the shore from Ellenabeich to Cuan. In the doctor's opinion the timber did more good for the health of the people by providing a decent blaze in their hearths that winter than ever it did in its hospital role! According to the *Oban Times* reporter, Dr Gillies also lost his boat on that occasion, a small price to pay perhaps in order to get the hospital building he coveted, the long-disused church at Cuan.

The Cuan church had been erected in 1732 when the two parishes of Kilbrandon and Kilchattan had been amalgamated under a single minister. The medieval church on the Isle of Luing had fallen into decay while that at Balvicar was too small to accommodate the steadily rising population of the slate quarrying villages. Following the Disruption of 1843, a number of new divisions of the church arose and smaller churches of different denominations were built in the district. In 1862, in an attempt to reunite the parishioners and to accommodate most of them in one building, Breadalbane provided the capital to build a new church in its present position at Kilbrandon, on the Cuan road. The old church at Cuan became redundant. In Patrick's estimation the abandoned building was the perfect solution to all his problems. Large enough to be subdivided into two wards, male and female, and with accommodation for laundry, food production and a live-in nurse, it was substantially built, in stone, to the highest standards of local construction and was conveniently positioned for all the islands in the parish.

After many delays and a great deal of wrangling over the details, by January 1902 Patrick was anticipating the opening of his hospital at Cuan. He begins his report for the year 1901:

The new fever hospital at Cuan will supply a long felt want in the parish. It is a handsome and substantial building giving ample accommodation both for patients and staff and providing every means of isolation and disinfection. It is centrally and conveniently situated, with a Southern exposure and having a gravitational supply of pure water. Sewage is easily disposed of in the sea, close by. The two wards have each a capacity of over 4000 cubic feet thus giving ample space for at least six beds. This structure is now completed and will soon be ready for occupation.

In the early days of Patrick's appointment there had been an air of prosperity about the quarry villages. Order books for slates were full, the great pits which had been dug to enormous depths below sea level, some as much as seventy metres, were yielding high-quality slates and the company was exporting four to five million slates a year. When the doctor was called out in an emergency it was most likely to attend an accident rather than any kind of sickness. His records indicate that confinements came second only to fractures, powder burns and concussions. Generally only the elderly and the very young required the services of a physician rather than a surgeon for at this time the rates of infant mortality were still very high and life expectancy rarely exceeded three score years and ten. Towards the end of the final decade of the nineteenth century however, the slate industry again fell into decline and slate sales slumped.

*The old church at Cuan which became Patrick's isolation hospital. Now a private house, it retains its original 'birdcage' belfry.*

Easdale slates were too hard to be cut by the machines recently introduced into the English and Welsh quarries to the south and as a consequence they could not compete for price with the cheaper imports. Financial backers began to pull out and several of the quarries ceased operation. Many of the men moved away, seeking jobs in the industrial Lowlands or in the gold fields of California, South Africa and Australia. Often they left their families behind until they had secured work and a new place to live. Needless to say, these families, lacking a working man's income, quickly began to experience dire poverty.

By 1897 enteric fever and tuberculosis, were appearing in epidemic proportions: the inevitable consequence of inadequate sanitation, overcrowded housing and poor diet. Patrick's 1901 report included this reference to the situation:

> As in previous years Typhoid fever has been endemic. Eleven cases occurred during the past twelve months. Of those, eight were directly or indirectly derived from Balvicar. One occurred in Toberonochy and another in Cullipool. The origin of these could not be determined and both the houses were very clean and well kept. The remaining case was that of a seaman who contracted the disease in New York and who came home to die. This was the only fatal case.
>
> The last three patients who suffered this disease during the year were isolated in the new isolation Hospital. No difficulty was experienced in their removal and from every point of view the experiment was most successful. I have already, in a letter to the District Clerk dated 18.12.01 given a statement of the names of patients, their period of detention and cost etc. of treatment.

Patrick had his way at last but, nevertheless, if the Lorn District Council thought that they had finally quieted this intense and determined young doctor, they were mistaken. His list of demands with regard to the hospital had only just begun.

The one particular problem which Patrick had so far failed to resolve was associated with the fact that the medical practice was distributed between parts of the mainland as well as three major and several minor island communities. This was the transportation of sick persons to the hospital from their homes. A mobile stretcher or ambulance, consisting of a two-wheeled chassis on which was constructed a stretcher covered in a canvas tent for protection against the weather, had been provided to medical practices throughout the county as standard equipment. Unfortunately this vehicle proved to be too wide to get onto the various ferry boats. In his report to the chief medical officer in 1910, Patrick discussed this problem and, as usual, provided his own solution: the contracting of open machines, either carriages or ferry boats. These, he felt,

*On Luing the pony trap was not only used as a passenger vehicle, it delivered the post and was on occasion used as an ambulance.*

were less prone to harbour infection, and provided patients with health-giving fresh air, as well as solving the problem of transport across the water. He went on to outline a number of other problems:

1. The absence of a mortuary. This is a very serious omission as a little consideration will show.
2. The want of an ash pit. This is absolutely necessary. [This was the forerunner of the clinker beds used in waste water cleansing in many sewage works today. As the foul water percolates through the ashes algae and oxygenating bacteria filter out and destroy the harmful bacteria in the waste.]
3. A minor defect is in the hot water apparatus. The kitchen range must be properly fitted as it is impossible to get the water in a large boiler anywhere near to boiling point.

In reports for the ensuing years there were several references to the isolation hospital at Cuan; many of them were congratulatory but others revealed the need for constant vigilance on the part of the doctor and not only in seeing that the county officials did their duty. In his report for 1906 Patrick records other matters of concern:

The coal house door of the hospital has been made secure. On several occasions this door was forced in. It has been invaded by scringers [scroungers] and considerable quantities of coals taken away. No proof could be got as to who were the depredators. The door has now been made to open outwards so that it will be more difficult for the offence to be repeated.

The hot water system in the hospital has been the cause of much trouble. It is frequently out of order and although plumbers have been employed on several occasions it is still unsatisfactory, the hot water pipe in the kitchen being periodically out of action.

Mr McConnel the short lease tenant of Ardmaddie [estate] in recognition of the value of the hospital in isolating several of his servants, who had contracted scarletina, gave a sum of five pounds [around five hundred pounds in today's terms] for the purchase of extra furniture. A very comfortable leather armed hospital couch was purchased and should prove a benefit for cases during convalescence. Apart from the ordinary wooden chairs there was no convenience of any kind whereby patients could recline. There is a small balance remaining. I propose to purchase a wicker easy chair therewith.

Having studied the sources of various outbreaks of typhoid in the district Patrick had by 1911 come to the conclusion that the disease was transmitted only by water or food contaminated by water. Over the years he had observed that certain groups of people, a family or a group of neighbours living in close proximity to one another, were the most likely to be the centre of any outbreak. Some houses over a period of twenty years, came to be expected to produce patients during the fever season. Having come to the conclusion that certain locations were themselves a source of infection and having, quite rightly, attributed this to the water supply, the obvious next step was to rectify the situation by demanding that landlords improve water supplies, particularly to the villages, but also to isolated farmhouses which were often the worst affected. Within the terms of the 1883 Local Government Act there was provision for the Sanitation Department to take action in cases of polluted water supplies, this was rarely done except by order of the chief medical officer for the county. As the number of instances of disease mounted, Patrick seemed constantly to be badgering the district medical officer.

Once typhoid had broken out there was a danger that the patient's body fluids might contaminate the food and drink of other members of the household. This could be controlled by carefully isolating the utensils used by the patient and ensuring proper disposal of all bodily wastes. Patrick carried out a campaign to educate the people by giving public lectures as well as instructing those actually caring for the sick in how to limit the spread of disease. But despite all these precautions, typhoid still occurred in households where the drinking water had been shown to be clear of contamination. In time, Patrick took to investigating the condition of the excreta of all members of a household in which one person had fallen sick. He then discovered that there were those who harboured the typhoid bacillus in their bodies while not presenting any symptoms of the disease itself. These 'carriers' he believed, could be responsible for outbreaks of fever where there was no other obvious reason for the disease to occur. If a carrier, as a result of careless personal hygiene, should contaminate food or drink consumed by another member of the household that person inevitably became sick.

On 1 Jan 1912 Patrick communicated his findings in a letter to the county clerk, J.D. Sutherland. By this time he had established his credentials as an expert on the subject of communicable disease. His words would not have been disregarded.

> As Dr. MacNeill D.M.O. has reported to you the advisability of examining the excreta of patients bacteriologically to eliminate or subdue the danger of 'carrier infection' I am retaining the girl MacNeill, who is also recovered recently and got the decision of your committee on the point. The girl, upon discharge, will go to a part of the parish which has not hitherto been affected with infection. It is essential (therefore) that I continue restricting her pending your investigation.
>
> The third patient is recovering rapidly and I hope to have the hospital free in the second week in February.
>
> Please let me hear from you with definite instructions of 'yes' or 'no' [presumably as to whether he may retain the girl] and upon the results of bacteriological tests upon patients in this area.

When the hospital had been in operation for its first decade it became clear that not everything was going according to plan. The caretaker, a woman who had been employed since the opening, had become slack in matters relating to the cleanliness of the premises and there was a constant battle concerning the proper use of materials supplied for the patients. For example, while her own room was kept warm, she skimped on the fires in the wards. Patrick became suspicious that all the money requisitioned for food for the patients was not being used for the purposes intended and there was the constant question of the disappearance of coals, a theft which he began to suspect was an 'inside job'. Whether well founded or not, his continuous complaints to the staff had created an uneasy atmosphere which he saw only one way to rectify. Early in 1912 Patrick was preparing to take up a new appointment with Argyll Council. As he wanted to leave everything in order for his successor he wrote to Mr Sutherland again, on 1 Feb, listing the changes he considered necessary in the general organisation of the hospital:

1.  The local medical officer must be appointed Medical Superintendent of the hospital with no salary but with fees for visiting patients as in the past. The present position is anomalous as I superintend the workings, send in returns accounts etc., without authorisation from the Local Authority.
2.  To give effect to the post, all nurses and servants must be subject to the authority of the Medical Superintendent. He alone will be responsible to the Local Authority for the correct and efficient administration of the hospital.
3.  A visiting committee of District Councillors should be appointed.
4.  All supplies where possible should be contracted for locally as getting these from Oban entails large expense for carriage or postage (see accounts for beef and poultry).

The services of the caretaker have of late been most unsatisfactory. I wish you to give her and other employees a month's notice to terminate their employment under the present regulations. They may be re-employed if it is seen fit and proper under the new conditions. I want these changes to take effect now as the continuance of the present system and present state of friction cannot continue.

Patrick's employers on the Lorn District Council had a history of being less than generous in recognising Patrick's activities regarding the hospital. In May 1911 he was obliged to protest the sum of money the authority were proposing to pay in fees for attendance upon hospitalised patients:

Dear Sir,

Referring to your letter of 19th April I regret I cannot accept the conditions laid down therein as my remuneration for attendance upon hospital patients.

It is not so much the remuneration itself which I object to; that has been ample in the past and ungrudgingly given as far as I know, but the fact that I am asked to go 3 miles or more to see a fever patient for the sum of two shillings and sixpence. This is not in accordance with the rules of my profession and I think when you consider that for the same distance the medical attendant to the Ballachulish Hospital gets seven shillings and sixpence, the treatment should be a like.

My offer is to attend the hospital from Dunmore, at seven shillings and sixpence per visit to the hospital, not per patient. I know that the expense will be no greater for this past year as we had a large number of patients. I should be the loser in this case but in the case of less than 3 patients I shall gain.

I might mention that in addition to the treatment of the sick. The work of superintending the administration of the hospital entails a considerable amount of work, clerical and otherwise. The giving of reports, the checking of accounts, the supervision of caretaker and nurses, the ordering of foods, medicines etc., all are undertaken. I think that a retaining fee should be allowed for this which is in no way a part of my duties but which I have hitherto done gladly and as faithfully as I could. Perhaps the committee can see their way in this connection to increase my salary as Local M.O.H., my work to include the above.

It is little wonder that there were members of the local authority who found the Easdale doctor tiresome. His arguments were, however, always sound. In his fight for his own rights and those of his fellow men, Patrick was not prepared to be hoodwinked or put down by penny-pinching bureaucrats. Doctoring in these circumstances was a hard business, offering little material reward and by 1911 Patrick had a growing family to support.

The scourge of typhoid, if not entirely eradicated from the district, had by this time been got under control. It was to be replaced very quickly by that of tuberculosis. Phthisical patients had cropped up from time to time during the days of Dr Hugh Gillies and Patrick had seen many cases during his time both in Edinburgh and Sheffield, but it had always been his contention that no tuberculin bacillus could withstand the rigorous climate of the Argyll coast. Indeed when asked to comment upon the provision of the new rotating chalets being recommended for the use of such patients he had suggested that all the family would be piling in along with the patient, to use them as bathing huts! To a great extent he was right to be sceptical because the treatment in those days was to expose the patient to fresh air in all weathers and no Easdale resident went short of that. By 1911, however, with the overcrowding, poor diet and miserable living conditions of many of his patients, Patrick began to see more and more cases of the disease. Without benefit of modern medication, in the late nineteen-hundreds the course of tuberculosis infection was a slow but steady decline usually resulting after some months in death. While the infectious nature of the disease was uncertain, Patrick considered that his phthisical patients required a warm environment, good food and adequate ventilation and that the best place for this was in his hospital. Unfortunately, the members of the district committee were never happy when patients lingered for any length of time in the hospital.

A boy suffering from a chest complaint which Patrick suspected of being a form of tuberculosis had been in the hospital for some weeks. Anticipating a complaint from the committee about his length of stay Patrick himself pointed out the case to the district clerk. It seems that at last he was beginning to see the value of using a little diplomacy when dealing with the bureaucrats.

J.D. Sutherland Esq.,                                Dunmore House, Easdale
                                                         30.10.1911

Dear Sir,

I enclose the monthly Hospital report. I am sorry to say that the boy, Livingstone, is not doing too well although I think he will get better and is recovering slowly. I have varied his diet in every way within the limits of my budget but with little success. He is nearly well but every few weeks he takes a relapse which lasts one week or there about. There is a possibility that the case may be drifting towards Tuberculosis but I hardly think so. Possibly a few weeks more may make him all right, but I feel the Committee may be getting weary. Perhaps you might ask Dr MacNeill to see the case along with me and decide upon the course to be followed. I have had Dr Campbell and Dr Currie seeing him already but perhaps it might be more satisfactory to the committee if one of their own officers saw him along with me.

The tuberculosis bacillus had for some time been recognised and would have shown up in sputum viewed under the microscope, if there was not yet any sign of the disease. Patrick's fear must have been based upon the thought that the boy's body was in so weak a state that he was prone to contract it.

Patrick, having been made wise by experience, knew that the committee would be much more likely to listen to the district medical officer, MacNeill, than to himself. Over the years he had had too many brushes with the authority over what they regarded as his extravagance in caring for his patients. They tended to calculate the actual cost of individuals treated in the hospital without having regard to the amount of money saved by preventing further spread of disease. Nevertheless, despite all the obstacles placed in his path, Patrick had achieved his aim of isolating infected patients, and until well into the twentieth century the little church at Cuan served the community as its fever hospital. Throughout the nineteen thirties and the Second World War, banishment to the fever hospital was still the only answer for those who succumbed to scarlet fever or diphtheria.

Typhoid was virtually eradicated from the district as sanitary arrangements improved although it was not until the 1950s that the first septic tank was installed on Easdale Island when a bakery opened at No.36, selling its products to the general public. As late as the 1980s, there were still a number of cottages in all the villages which were without running water and flushing toilets.

# 5 A School for Cullipool

LIKE HIS FATHER before him, Patrick was concerned not only for the health of the people he served but for every aspect of life in the community. When he returned for a second time to the Easdale practice in 1894, it was to find himself in the midst of political conflict and the parish in a state of turmoil over the future of its educational provision. The larger proportion of the parishioners were incensed that certain of their elected representatives, with the backing of a small minority of the community, were attempting to save public money by depriving the majority of what few benefits they had managed to obtain through the introduction of various reforming Acts of Parliament passed during the previous two decades. Among their plans was a proposal to do away with one of the four schools in the parish, that at Cullipool. How could it be that so small a number of the people could affect the lives of so many without their having any say in the matter?

The Local Government Act of 1883 extended the franchise to those owning property producing an income of ten pounds a year or more. In order to defray the cost of public services such as street cleaning and refuse disposal, maintenance of roads, the provision of certain public health services and education, these property owners were obliged to pay a certain portion of this income to the Local Authority in the form of rates and hence described themselves as the ratepayers. The vast majority of the population of the Slate Islands were quarrymen and farm labourers working for wages and occupying houses rented from their employers. Having no property of their own which might produce any

The class of c.1900 at Easdale School with the headmaster Mr Stewart and his assistant.
It was the inadequate clothing of some children, their lack of footwear and their general
debility which first alerted Patrick to the need for some form of supervision. His concerns

resulted in the establishment of regular medical inspections of the school children, which included sight and hearing tests and an assessment of general hygiene as well as suitability of clothing.

kind of income, they had no vote either in parish or in county council affairs. They were entirely in the hands of the very few ratepayers in the district.

Patrick had been taught by his father and by his strict Christian upbringing, to concern himself with the welfare of all his fellow men no matter how lowly their status. There was no way in which the young doctor could continue to perform his duties under these circumstances while ignoring what was going on. His first instinct was to turn to the pen as a means of drawing the attention of those outside the district to the plight of the disadvantaged majority of Easdale. He wrote several drafts of a letter to the *Oban Times* but common sense was to stay his hand when it came to applying a signature to his note. Despite his late father's high standing in the community, it was now up to Patrick to re-establish the Easdale Medical Practice at Dunmore and he was not so foolish as to antagonise at the outset those wealthier members of the community who might constitute his fee-paying patients! Consequently his letter to the *Oban Times* appeared under the nom de plume of Miss Susan MacLaggan. This copy letter appears in his letter book, clearly written in the doctor's own hand. The letter appears to be a follow-up of previous publications in the *Oban Times* written by a Mr Bloggs (also a nom de plume) and OUR TRIO, representing the quarrymen.

### Cullipool School, Civil War at Easdale

If the old saying, happy the people whose annals are vacant be true then is Kilbrandon and Kilchattan the most unhappy of parishes. Each succeeding year brings its fresh burden of quarrel and bitterness. Every season yields a luxuriant crop of discord and enmity, the struggle between labourer and employer, between classes and masses waxes finer and finer while the increasing amount of issues at stake and the personal nature of the quarrel in many cases add fuel to the fire and rancour to the strife.

The Cullipool School question is but one entry in a large index but it elucidates the present position of parochial history. We find the two opposing forces of ratepayers and quarriers or to be more precise, ratepayers and labourers, fighting not for a school in Cullipool, that is but a stage on the road, but for supremacy, nay for very existence as factors in government of the parish.

While the ratepayers are few in number they are well armed with edged weapons: multiple votes. The labour party make up for their weaponless condition by their numbers, unity, enthusiasm and trustful faith in future legislation: one man, one vote on our parish councils. The policy of the former is based upon the principle of active aggression and 'no surrender' while the latter maintains a stubborn attitude of passive but potent resistance.

In an age like the present when the reconsideration of many laws and the problems of government is inevitable, and when the people, those *comunit menaces* which M Bloggs speaks of, have more power and a larger and increasing voice in the discussion than at any previous period; in this age of reform when even Socialism, Communism and

Fourierism [the idea, drawing much public interest at the time, that society could be reorganised into self-sufficient units, with conventional living arrangements, marriage and property ownership all redesigned] are possibilities I may be forgiven if I express my doubts of the wisdom of the ratepayers policy. Could they but consider the past they should find that this policy of 'no surrender' this inability to compromise has usually heralded the downfall of the party which practised it. If the electors were left to themselves I should expect them to show more perception and forethought but unfortunately they are badly guided.

Ratepayers of this parish, as a class, resemble their neighbours the quarriers in one respect. They are easily led. To be a perfect leader one requires a certain amount of theatrical display, loud bombast and blundering ignorance. These qualities have for long adorned the leaders of the quarrymen: 'OUR TRIO' for instance. But it is only of late that prophets possessed of such attributes have risen amongst us to lead the ratepayers to victory. Prophets who by their pantomime buffoonery and brazen effrontery have assumed the place of better men and dazzled all by their blandishments.

I am yours truly, Susan MacLaggan

This letter to the newspaper brought an immediate reaction from the minority group on the school board, at least one member of which must have recognised the hand holding the pen because, although not yet elected to the board, Patrick was asked to take a hand in a bitter dispute which was raging within its confines. This was the matter of the requirement to provide four schools within the parish boundaries.

The majority group, concerned to save money, had decided that, having already established three of the new school buildings planned for the parish, there was no necessity to build a fourth, at Cullipool. This decision had been arrived at despite the fact that the population of Cullipool was equal to that of any of the other villages and that the existing school, although well equipped, was housed in a temporary building. The school had received the highest praise from the government inspector on his annual visit in 1893 so it could not be closed on grounds of inefficiency.

In May 1894, before he himself could be elected either to the parish council or the school board, Patrick was prevailed upon by a Mr McInnis to compose a suitable letter of protest to the Secretary of State for Education (Scotland).

Although written by Patrick, the letter was signed by Arthur McInnis:

Sir,

In the name of the inhabitants of Cullipool I beg to tender the department their sincerest thanks for the establishment of a properly equipped school in the village of Cullipool.

I have been asked to inform you that the school has been, so far, a thorough success. There are 46 children on the roll. We have an energetic and popular teacher and so far the School Board and the people of Cullipool have worked harmoniously together in the cause and for the success of the school.

While thus acknowledging our indebtedness to the Department we regret to inform you that the initial term of office of this School Board being about to expire, a determined effort is being made by a section of the ratepayers to oust, at the coming election, any candidate favourable towards the Cullipool School. Their efforts may not meet with success but should they do so, it is our cause which will suffer and we take this opportunity of appealing to you and earnestly beseeching the Department to be our friends and benefactors in the future as in the past. Please deal with us leniently and treat with a firm hand any movement originated with the intention of suppressing the school.

Arthur McInnis

Tempers generally were running high by this time. Perhaps egged on by Patrick's open defiance of the parish councillors, there followed a spate of letters in the *Oban Times*, some politely remonstrating, others downright insulting as was one signed 'Bauldy Beg' complaining that the parish councillors were wasting public money by holding their meetings at different places around the extensive parish and claiming their travelling expenses for doing so. The writer suggested that this was an indication of a greater interest in the councillors' comfort and entertainment than in the business they met to conduct.

It was a courageous being who dared to take up the cudgels in such an acrimonious atmosphere, but Patrick Hunter Gillies had never in his life stood back when there was fighting to be done. He knew that if he was going to tackle these ratepayers on their own ground, he would have to become elected to the parish council and to the school board himself. His mother had been a ratepayer from the outset but as soon as he became a permanent resident at Dunmore, Patrick took upon himself the mantle of 'Head of the Household' and therefore qualified both as a voter and to stand for election. In May 1894, when Patrick became a candidate for election to the parish council, the following, to the parish minister, is one of his letters asking for support from the electorate.

To the very reverend Mr MacDonald and Mrs MacDonald

Dear Sir and Madam,

I hope I shall have the honour of having at least a share of your support at the coming election.

Although only landowners and substantial lease holders held the franchise at this time, they were entitled to additional votes according to the number of subtenants or servants in their charge. Such voters could cast a number of votes and not necessarily for only one candidate.

After a few personal pleasantries Patrick goes on to say:

I believe you have a fair idea of my views on certain aspects of island matters and if they meet with your approbation I trust that some of your votes may come to me.

I am Sir, yours faithfully

Patrick H Gillies

Patrick, partly because of his father's reputation but also undoubtedly as a result of his own activities in the parish, was elected to the parish council in 1894 with a substantial number of votes and, despite many altercations with other members throughout the years, he held this position until he left the district in 1912. Within four years he was also honoured by being invited to become a justice of the peace, a role he was to continue to fulfil until his death in 1931.

On being elected to the parish council it seems that the doctor immediately landed himself with the job of secretary to the finance committee, possibly an attempt to place him on the side of those determined to save the ratepayers money at all costs. He was soon to discover, unfortunately, that the finance committee had no executive powers. Within weeks of his accession to the post he found he must write to a local contractor cancelling a contract for the maintenance to Achafolla School, a deal he had inadvertently made off his own bat :

Dunmore Easdale 19.09.1894

To Mr Don MacKay, Contractor
Clachan

Dear Sir,

While talking about Kilgour's contract for interior work of the Achafolla School I was under the impression that the [School] Board had given us power to accept the contract without further meeting. I am informed that this is not so. Such being the case and seeing that as a Finance Committee we have not been endowed with too much power I think it would be more regular to defer the matter until next meeting. As far as I can see such is the proper course and the one which I should adopt. Should we do otherwise we lay ourselves open to blame.

I am yours faithfully,

Patrick H Gillies

In accordance with the 1873 Education Act, school boards were also elected and the minutes of a meeting of Kilchrenan and Dalavich School Board of

1900 indicates clearly the process by which these elections were conducted. Unlike the parish councils, school boards were in receipt of a direct grant from central government in Whitehall. For this reason they acted independently of local government at least until the reforms of the Local Government Acts of the early twentieth century. They were answerable directly to the 'Scotch' Education Department in Whitehall, as it then called itself, and were forced to exercise certain constraints and meet certain requirements if they expected to receive the full grant from the government. Other finance was provided as in the past, partly by the parish council and also by local subscription. The clerk to the board, a local government official, was the convener and the returning officer for elections to the board. Notice of an election was placed in designated places around the parish. Names of nominees, supported by five names from among the electors, were posted prior to the election date and polling took place in the various schools in the parish.

The Easdale District School Board which was elected in 1894 consisted of five members, three of which were those same gentlemen who had raised so much ire by their determination to do away with the Cullipool School. The fourth was the proprietor of the Tigh an Truish Inn at Clachan, Seil, Mr Norman Weir, and the fifth was Dr Patrick Gillies. Weir, like Patrick, supported the majority working class of the district and the two men immediately formed an alliance which was to last for many years.

When Weir and Gillies took their places on the school board they were immediately confronted with what appeared to be a *fait accompli*. The school closure had already been announced and the schoolmaster had received his notice to quit. When the Education Scotland Act of 1873 was first implemented, the Secretary of State for Education had laid down that there should be four schools in the parish positioned in the four main centres of population. These were the quarry villages of Ellenabeich, both Toberonochy and Cullipool on Luing, and Ardencaple, a large estate peopled by agricultural workers and including the scattered community in the proximity of the Tigh an Truish Inn at Clachan, Seil.

Within four years sufficient funds had been raised by public subscription and augmented by government grants to build three fine buildings, two of which remain in use as public schools to this day. These were at Ardencaple, Easdale and Achafolla, a mile or two to the north of Toberonochy. The fourth school, at Cullipool, was housed in an existing substantial stone building, the

Volunteers' drill hall, which served also as the community hall. Some attempt had been made to convert it to a school building but only as a temporary measure until such time as a purpose-built school could be provided. From 1890 onwards, the slate industry having fallen into some decline, a number of families had left the district and by 1894 the Cullipool school roll had fallen somewhat. The parish councillors had seized upon this fact to substantiate their decision to close the school, thereby saving the cost of a full-time schoolmaster and a female assistant as well as ridding themselves of the burden of raising further monies for a new school building.

When the matter was reviewed at the first meeting of the school board attended by Weir and Gillies these two gentlemen protested forcibly. They were of course outvoted by the ratepayers group and it was quite clear that when the proposal to close the school was put to the next full meeting of the parish council the decision to close the school would be upheld. Not to accept their defeat without a fight, Weir and Gillies decided to make the minority view of the board known to the secretary to the Board of Education.

Honoured Sir,

As you are aware, the School Board of the Kilbrandon and Kilchattan Parish have determined by a majority of 3 to 2, to reduce the fully equipped school (at Cullipool) established by order of the Board of Education, to the status of an infants school.
We desire in the name of the people of Cullipool to protest against the action of the School Board in this matter. In the school, which the Board of Education approved, the children are taught to the sixth standard. A competent teacher Mr Patterson acted as master and the present building was engaged temporarily all with your approval for the purpose of a test being made.
If the present teacher, one of the factors in your fully equipped school, be dismissed and a pupil teacher substituted we cannot see how the test of your school can be carried out. In short, the actions of the previous board are set at nought and your suggestions and recommendations which were issued and carried out after full and careful deliberation have been defied.
We are afraid, indeed it is almost certain, that The Board in their action are not acting in a straight forward manner. They propose continuing the infant school only as long as the Board of Education allow the hall to be used as such. Should new buildings be requested the board are prepared to stop the school entirely. The salary of the new pupil teacher is fixed at £50.00 per annum with no share of the grant, a sum evidently meant to discourage applications. It seems only too likely that the intention is to do away with the school at the earliest possible moment and to take the least contentious way of effecting this purpose.
The step will doubtless please a certain section probably the poorer and more ignorant of the ratepayers but when we consider that ratepayers and their families form only one twentieth part of the parish as a whole and that at the last election out of a total vote of 450, the majority of those voting wanted the school left as it is, we cannot

see that the school board has much support from the rest of the parish. In effect they have made the fight one of party politics and not in the interests of education.

Of course in this matter we are helpless. We must look to the Board of Education for aid and for a guarantee that their orders and suggestions, which the late board put into force shall continue to be carried out. We therefore pray you, My Lords, to intervene and to compel the local board to do their duty; to compel them to reinstate the present teacher who has been their unwitting victim; to retain the school as it stands at present, fully equipped, and if after the set period of trial the result goes against us and the school proves a failure, we will then be ready to submit to your decision as we have done in the past.

This letter, written in Patrick's hand is nevertheless signed by that same McInnis who had signed the previous letter. This gentleman must still have been a member of the parish council although perhaps no longer a member of the school board.

At the October meeting of the school board the resolution was indeed passed, by a majority vote of only one, to disband the Cullipool school. The clerk was instructed to inform the secretary to the Board of Education of this decision. Patrick and his friend Weir wrote again, on 20 October 1894, this time under their own signatures, to Whitehall to apprise the education secretary of this decision and to place before him their own minority report.

Sir, I enclose an extract from the minutes of the school Board entered at a meeting held at Achafolla, Luing, on the 15th inst. A clerk was instructed to record only the resolution of the majority of the Board but I have thought it advisable to give the department details of the entire minute so that they may be fully informed of the state of affairs:

16th Oct. 1894
Copy of a petition sent by Cullipool Committee.
The petition of the undersigned humbly showed that at the meeting of the school Board of Kilbrandon and Kilchattan yesterday, October 15th 1894, it has been decided by a majority of one that the fully equipped school at Cullipool be put down and that it be reduced to an infant school.

That the present teacher has been warned that he will be dismissed on November 9th.

That the evening classes which were opened have been closed and that the whole state of educational matters in Cullipool are definitely on the down grade once more.

That we, the undersigned, desire in the name of the people of Cullipool to protest against the actions and decisions of the board, but that as we are sensitive of our helplessness in this matter we must look to the Board of Education for aid and pray that my Lords interfere and impel the school board to do its duty.

That as we have no other means of freeing ourselves from this evil but by appealing to your department we hope that my lords will look favourably upon our grievance and upon we your humble petitioners:

Patrick H Gillies, Norman Weir

This petition brought an immediate response, in the form of a letter to the clerk to the school board. On 23 Oct 1894 J. Shute Robertson wrote to the clerk to Easdale School Board to inform him that 'my Lords are not at present prepared to consent to the proposal of your Board to reduce the school at Cullipool to the status of an infant school.' This seems remarkable to us in these days, when letters to such authorities often take weeks to elicit an answer.

This reply to the Clerk of the Kilbrandon and Kilchattan School Board, which enclosed, for the information of the board as a whole, the petition of Weir and Gillies, made it very clear that the secretary of state agreed with Patrick and his friend. As far as Patrick was concerned he felt they had won a great victory. In his letter book he wrote: 'Kilbrandon and Kilchattan School Board. Victory of the Department … The Board cave in!' He then went on to copy into his book a word by word account of all that took place at the meeting which followed receipt of the reply from the ministry in Whitehall:

> The chairman brought before the notice of the Board the following letter [13 Nov] received from the department regarding Cullipool School [. . .]
>
> 'I have the honour to acknowledge the receipt of your letter of the 5th inst. I am to state that after communicating with HM Inspector my Lords adhere to the view expressed in their letter of 23rd October.'

Patrick and Norman Weir could not help but rejoice in the discomfort of their fellow members of the board. It must have been with a certain amount of irony that Norman Weir laid the following motion on the table:

> That the Board, having before them the Education Department's decision refusing to sanction the reduction of the Cullipool School and having in view the fact that the attendance at the said school seems to be such as would warrant it being fully supported and for the securing of the grants to recoup the Board for the heavy expenses already incurred in this direction: and in the interest of education generally throughout the period, this Board do heartily concur in the department's findings. It is therefore necessary that this Board advertise immediately for Cullipool School and further crave the department's sanction to allow the school to be kept open by a pupil teacher until such time as a fully qualified teacher is secured: and in this way to meet the requirements of the code for the purpose of securing the full grant.

The chairman, although clearly affronted, was determined not display his annoyance in front of Gillies and Weir. He indicated that he would himself be glad to second the motion provided Mr Weir agreed to certain amendments. Gillies sensing some devilry was intended, intervened by agreeing to second the motion himself.

The chairman then declared that the motion as read was 'quite incompetent' and refused to put it to the meeting. When Mr Weir demanded to know what was incompetent about what he had written the chairman replied, 'Because you are stating as facts what has no foundation; for instance you speak in the name of the Board and you make the Board concur heartily with the Department, a statement which considering our past proceedings, is quite ridiculous. Again, you say the school will be self supporting. You cannot prove that.'

'It is not necessary for me to prove my statement,' Weir protested. 'It is for the meeting to show where I was wrong.' The chairman's reply was petulant. 'As Chairman I can refuse to entertain any motion that I please and unless you can see your way to alter it I shall refuse to put this motion to the meeting.'

At this point Dr Gillies intervened. 'If only motions approved by the majority are accepted,' he suggested, 'it is useless for the minority to exist. The motion submitted by Mr Weir is perfectly competent and bears out our view on the question. The proper and judicious course is for the chairman to allow Mr Weir's motion and then he can move any amendment he pleases.'

So far Weir and Gillies had had things their own way. Now it was the turn of the opposition in the form of a Mr Mackay.

'I am inclined to support the Chairman. It is high time that this unprincipled and extraordinary opposition on the part of the minority should cease. It is only by their action in supporting the Department that the majority of the Board has had to cave in. I for one am determined that no motion of theirs shall find its way into the minutes of the Board for publication.'

This statement gives a clear indication of just how unprincipled were these members who called themselves the Ratepayers Party. The democratic process implies that all opinions be heard and recorded for publication. Gillies could see little point in the chairman's argument. 'It is foolish,' he maintained, 'for the majority to use their power in such an arbitrary fashion particularly when the views of the minority have been confirmed by the Department.'

But Mr Mackay was adamant: 'We have the majority and we will use our power,' he declared belligerently.

'Go on then,' Weir challenged him.

At this point Mr Shaw intervened, his milder manner pouring a little oil on the troubled waters. 'Allow me have a look at the motion,' he suggested. 'There are some things here which I really do not feel I can go along with. Besides which, I think we have to agree with our Chairman.'

For the board to have disagreed with the chairman would have been to pro-pose a motion of no confidence in him and might even have required a new election, a position which would put the entire board in a bad light.

Weir was determined however. 'I refuse most emphatically to alter one word of my original motion,' he insisted.

While this discourse continued the chairman had been scribbling rapidly on the pad of paper in front of him. At last, conscious that the discussion had come to an abrupt halt, he lifted his head. 'I am sorry we cannot be unanimous in this,' he said, casting a leering grimace which might have been taken from a triumphant smile, at the pair who remained in the minority. 'There is so very little to quarrel about. A little consideration on the part of the minority would show them where things are unreasonable. I have drafted a motion here which should meet the requirements of us all. It is as follows:

> That in order to ensure the grant from the Education department a female certified teacher be appointed for a salary of £45 per year, capable of teaching sewing and singing to take up duties immediately. Meantime Miss MacQueen (pupil teacher) be requested to teach the school till the new teacher comes.

Looking up with a bland expression he then declared: 'I think Mr Weir should move this motion.'

But Mr Weir would have none of it. 'No,' he said, 'I stick to my first motion.'

With a sigh the Chairman turned to his right-hand man, 'Well, Mr Mackay, you had better move this then, if you will.'

Mr Mackay's reply was entirely predictable. 'Of course, Mr Chairman, I have great pleasure in moving it.'

Mr Shaw seconded the motion which was carried without dissent, there being nothing in it with which Gillies and Weir could disagree.

The clerk was instructed to advertise for a teacher, replies with testimonials to be in by 12th December. This was all the business of the meeting.


To the last, Dr Gillies and Mr Weir adhered to their own motion and made a formal protest that it had not been taken to a vote and consequently would not appear in the minutes. But their point had been made and there was little doubt that there were those amongst the company would be unable to keep a still tongue in their heads when it came to regaling dinner guests with the latest tittle-tattle to emerge from the dealings of the parish council! Patrick's was to

Patrick's battle to keep the school at Cullipool open was clearly successful as this 1940s photograph indicates. The children attended school here from age 5 to 10 then moved on to the school at Achafolla near Toberonochy, walking the 3 miles there and back every day. Most of them remained until age 13. Those children bright enough to win a scholarship, went on to Oban High School where they might remain until they were 16. Tuition for these children was free but not every parent could afford to pay for the school uniform.

prove a hollow victory however. Fate, in the form of the failing slate quarrying industry, was soon to give the school board every reason to close the Cullipool School. By 1900, so many families had left the island of Luing that the board could legitimately claim there were insufficient senior pupils to justify more than one school on the island. The Cullipool School, still in its original building, was reduced to an infants' school with a female teacher. At the age of seven years the remaining Cullipool and Port St Mary children were obliged to walk the three miles to Achafolla daily.

One of these hardy pupils was Angus Shaw, whose uncle managed the quarries on Belnahua and whose father was a substantial property owner on Luing. In his mid eighties this gentleman, one time Editor of the *Glasgow Evening News*, recalled running to Achafolla school through bog and heather without shoes during the summer months and on Sundays walking sedately with his parents to the ferry at South Cuan to attend church on the Isle of Seil.

There were many further occasions when Patrick Gillies clashed with those who felt his demands for improvements both in the schools and elsewhere amongst the poor of the parish were too extravagant. As the local doctor he was also a member of the committee administering the Poor Law, bringing to the meetings his firsthand evidence of the parlous state of many of the parishioners. Arguments in council meetings sometimes became heated and words were spoken which could not be condoned. As this letter of 26 May 1905 suggests, he was not without enemies and, when need arose, he dealt with them accordingly.

Ballachuan House, Easdale

Dear Mr Owen,

I enclose my account for medical attendance upon your household during the last six months.

I much regret that owing to recent events (particularly your unwarranted conduct towards me at the last Board meeting) I do not wish to have any intercourse with you professionally or otherwise in the future and merely intimate this to you to save you any inconvenience. As there is another medical man in the parish I do not feel that I am imposing any hardship upon you or taking advantage of my position. As you believe my friendship is of no value to you (you indicated as much in the private talk after the meeting) and as your friendship is certainly valueless to me, I am quite content that in the future we should be entire strangers.

Yours very truly,

Patrick H Gillies

While his concerns as a member of the school board were in the main with the condition of the school buildings and the maintenance of standards of education, Patrick could not fail to notice the steady decline in attendances during those periods when work was scarce and every penny earned by child labour in the fields or quarries was required to keep the family going. Nor could he ignore the increase in incidences of children arriving at school, ill clothed, underfed and often suffering from the results of poverty and overcrowding. Such conditions as impetigo, head lice and infectious diseases of all kinds manifested themselves during this period. How, he demanded of his colleagues on the board, could children be expected to learn when they were too hungry to concentrate and in some cases too tired to stay awake in lessons?

By 1910, when the threat of poverty, even eviction, hung over the villages in the Slate Islands like a black pall, Patrick began to formulate his ideas for universal improvements in the condition of school children. He wanted to ensure that all children of school age were properly fed and adequately clothed and had plenty of fresh air and exercise. In such circumstances, he declared, they would approach their lessons with open and retentive minds. To those who threw up their hands in horror at such extravagant ideas he pointed out how much society, in particular employers of the labouring classes, would benefit from an alert, well-educated workforce. For two years he pursued this theme, speaking on the subject at public meetings, and writing to the learned journals and the popular press. In 1911 he presented to the chief medical officer for Argyll a paper for discussion by the members of the county council, 'On the Medical Inspection of School Children'. It was a move which two years later was to change his life dramatically.

# 6 The Farm at Dunmore

ALTHOUGH HIS PRIMARY interests were always the health and welfare of his patients, the family farm was never far from Patrick's thoughts and for most of his life he took a managerial role if not a practical hand its operation. When Jessie Gillies was left a widow with a young family to support it had been the farm which sustained her until her children were able to provide for themselves. The farm had been her sole source of income while she put the children through school and the sacrifices she made in order to pay for Hugh's naval apprenticeship and Patrick and Hugh's university education must have been very great indeed. It is little wonder that Patrick felt obliged to help run the farm by overseeing its finances and dealing with its business affairs on behalf of his mother and eventually his brothers also.

The present Dunmore House, of late eighteenth-century construction, has changed little over the years and is still the principal building on the Dunmore estate. Today the land is given over principally to sheep and the rearing of game birds, supplying those Scottish estates which rely upon their grouse moors for their income. In Patrick's day the bottom land was given over to fodder crops and dairy cattle while sheep grazed the slopes of Ben Mor. Sub-tenants, who occupied the subsidiary farms of Cairnban and An Grianan, grew sufficient crops for their own use as well as providing labour for the home farm.

The first Dunmore House had been built during the sixteenth century by the second son of the Duke of Argyll, the Captain of Ardmaddy Castle. This gentleman, having married for convenience, found his wife to be an

Dunmore was typical of farms in the area. On the valley floor alluvial soil supported grain crops, mainly oats and barley, which could be raised and harvested more successfully than wheat in the short growing season. Turnips and other fodder crops were grown to feed stock during the winter and considerable acreage was given over to grass, which could be cut for hay. Sheep grazed the steeper slopes, being raised in the first instance for wool; animals were only slaughtered for meat after several lambing and sheering seasons. Dunmore raised some dairy as well as store cattle and Jessie Gillies' dairy products were sold throughout the district. Although the wealthier tenant farmers occupied larger

houses such as Dunmore, the sub-tenants and agricultural labourers lived, until well into the twentieth century, in small, ill-ventilated cottages, sharing part of the ground floor with their animals in the winter months. Sanitation was for the most part absent. Water came from a well or nearby burn, which was often contaminated. It was not uncommon for a family of six or more to occupy a one-roomed hovel. In the right foreground is the manse, occupied in the 1880s by the Rev. MacIntyre, whose daughter Mary Davinia MacIntyre was to become Patrick's wife.

encumbrance to his more amorous activities. He eventually entered into a biga-
mous marriage with his cousin, who was also a Campbell, and Dunmore House
was built to accommodate his lawful spouse. For this transgression, the Duke of
Argyll, who administered the law in the County of Argyll, fined his son twenty
thousand pounds [around three hundred thousand pounds today] and banished
him from the country, his property being forfeit to his cousin, Campbell of
Breadalbane. Although the legal spouse was allowed to remain in Dunmore
House until her death, the property, together with Ardmaddy and all of the
Slate Islands, was placed in the hands of the Breadalbane Campbells. There it
remained until the dissolution of the Breadalbane estates in the 1930s.

It is not known exactly when the original house fell into such disrepair that
it had to be demolished, but a new building was erected on the original foundations late in the eighteenth century. The new Dunmore House, which still
stands, was built to the highest standards in the tradition of the period, under a
slated, gabled roof. Tall windows overlook the bay, commanding a fine view of

*Dunmore meadow from the house. Crops grown here were mainly fodder for the stock, turnips
and kale. Latterly Jessie Gillies planted here, the barley used in distilling, and supplied the
Easdale distillery. It proved the most profitable of all her crops.*

*The view eastwards towards the steading at Cairnban. Cattle grazed the valley floor, while sheep roamed across the hillsides.*

the distant islands. This generous fenestration and the finely moulded cornices, which remain unaltered to this day, suggest considerable expenditure at the time of its construction.

A series of large public rooms lead off a small entrance hall from which a gently curving staircase with fine, wrought-iron balustrade, gives access to the upper rooms. The kitchen and dining room are sufficient to accommodate a sizeable family and to entertain visitors when needs be. The dairy and out-houses, which were situated close by, would have been convenient for Jessie as would the adjacent stables for the horses: the doctor's pony for the trap and a sprightly hunter for longer trips on horseback across the hills, as well as the two heavy-duty draft horses which worked on the farm.

Despite some additions and alterations, mainly incurred during conversion in the 1950s to a small hotel, the older part of the house is little changed from the day the Gillies family moved in, in 1873. It was a grand residence for a country doctor and his family.

John had been only thirteen years of age when his father died but he rose valiantly to the occasion by trying to lift some of the burden of running the farm from his mother's shoulders. He matured quickly and was soon able to take on some of the work of the hired labourers thereby saving Jessie money.

It was unfortunate that during the first few years of Jessie's widowhood the slate industry fell steadily into decline. The situation created a period of serious recession throughout the district and it affected the farm at Dunmore particularly badly. With the quarries out of action, the manager had disposed of the horses employed to haul wagons of slate from the quarries. There was no sense in having these great lumbering Clydesdales and Suffolk Punches munching the quarry owners out of house and home when there was no work for them to do! Suddenly, fodder crops, introduced to the farm by Jessie and supplied to the quarries in a lucrative contract, were no longer required. At the same time, many families left the district to find other work and the demand for dairy products dropped alarmingly, while on the open market the price of wool and mutton had fallen to rock bottom.

Unable to continue to pay the rent which had been agreed to by Hugh Gillies when the family had been receiving a doctor's income, his widow approached the estate manager, Mr Duncan, for an interview with Breadalbane himself. She and Hugh had always had an easy relationship with the earl and she felt that faced directly with her predicament he might find it difficult to refuse to help her. The interview was refused however and she had to resort to a letter:

Dunmore House                                              16th August 1889

To the Most Noble the Marquis of Breadalbane

My Lord,

I am sorry that it is impossible for your lordship to grant me an interview as it would be much easier for me to explain the position of my affairs in that way than by writing.
I have written Mr Duncan giving an offer for the (rent of the) farm. As I find it impossible to make the farm pay with the present rent I have offered a portion of the money only.
I would beg Your Lordship to consider my case favourably as we have been your Lordship's tenants on the one farm for the last twenty five years and it is only within the last three years that we have been in arrears.
    As Your Lordship knows, farmers have suffered greatly from the bad market for the last few years but in addition I, like the other Netherlorn farmers, have felt greatly the depression which has existed in the slate trade here ever since 1882. Indeed my income from the dairy has fallen to almost nothing. It is now at least a fifth what it used to be. Without horses working the quarries, they do not require oats and ryegrass as usual and otherwise there is no sale. I wish I could have shown Your Lordship my bank book account and explained matters much more fully.
    In conclusion would Your Lordship kindly consider the following offer [a space was left here, in this copy letter]. Grant me a lease at the above mentioned rent for five years and I will bind myself to clear all the arrears but then, if things improve, I will be very glad to enter into a longer lease under a new arrangement.

I am Your Lordship's most obedient servant

Janet Gillies

His lordship clearly felt some compassion for the widow woman who had struggled so bravely to maintain her family. Jessie did indeed manage to sign a lease for a further five years on her own terms. When it terminated in 1894 Patrick became the leaseholder in his mother's stead and retained that position until the family relinquished both house and farm in 1919.

In the following years Jessie Gillies and her sons became respected as farmers throughout the district. Their stock commanded good prices at market and they won many prizes at the various agricultural shows held annually through-out the county. Only when the general economy of the area declined did Patrick find it necessary to write again on Jessie's behalf to the earl, now Mar-quess of Breadalbane, for a reduction in the rent.

Dunmore House Easdale
Sept 11th 1894

To William Dunn Esq.
Breadalbane Estate Office, Kenmore

Dear Sir,

I duly received your letter of the 6th inst. In it you ask how I intend making up the arrears of rent amounting in all to £397.

When arranging the last lease I had promised to pay these arrears in half yearly instalments. I am sorry that I have found it impossible to do so times having gone from bad to worse and it will be hard to fulfil any bargain unless lenient. With a reduction in rent and an improvement in my current circumstances otherwise, I think it will be possible with a little concession on his Lordship's part to pay off these arrears. Of course I must acknowledge the debt, it is a just one, but I am certain no one will say I trespass upon his Lordship's kindness when I ask for 25% to be cut off as these arrears began and increased during a period of almost unequalled depression and while I was paying an overly high rent.

If this be granted I will bind myself to get sufficient security to pay yearly the sum of £50 at least. I hope you can give me a ten year's lease with a break at the end of five years, the lease to include my own name and that of my sons John and Thomas. I hope you will let me have his lordship's decision in this matter as soon as possible.

Having made this entreaty on his mother's behalf, Patrick could not resist the temptation to put in a few demands of his own:

You may remember it was understood that if I got a new lease the south west wall of the dwelling house would be pointed. This is absolutely necessary for the preservation of the interior. Mr Fisher has doubtless written to you about the fences. The march

*Dunmore farmhouse was constructed during the latter half of the eighteenth century. It was occupied by Jessie's farm manager for most of the year, but in the summer months the family moved in, to leave Dunmore House free for summer visitors, a useful source of additional income.*

fence is in your hands but as I have agreed to erect the fence separating the arable and grazing lands and as Mr Fisher may not have understood, I wish it to be a corriemonie with iron standards and barbed wire on top. If Lord Breadalbane will supply the materials I will engage to have it erected to your satisfaction at my own expense. There are some fences out of repair. Could the tenant not get a few stobs from Ardmaddy to repair them?

The letter was no doubt signed by Jessie but the copy (in his letter book) is written in Patrick's unmistakable hand.

True to her word, Jessie made changes to both her crop programme and her animal stocks in order to ensure that she would be able to fulfil her promise to the marquis. She planted bere, a variety of barley used in the production of whisky. This was sold on contract to the distilleries at Easdale and Oban. She decreased her dairy cattle and concentrated for a time on store cattle, which she sold in the Oban market, and she increased her output of wool, a product which could, if necessary, be stored until the markets improved.

Despite the fact that his departure would cost her the wages of another man on the farm, Jessie also kept her promise to allow John to spread his wings by making a trip to Canada in 1884 when he was seventeen. When, eighteen months later, things began to get more difficult on the farm, she recalled him in order to save on the wages paid for casual labour. After a short spell in America, John returned to Easdale and remained until the farm began to recover. Then he was off again, this time to try his luck, first in the Falkland Islands and then in New Zealand. To Jessie's relief, John returned to Easdale after only two years abroad, and he took up a job with their neighbour, Mr Robertson of Kilbride Farm.

*Kilbride farmhouse where John Gillies worked on his return from the Falkland Isles and New Zealand.*

During John's absences abroad, with Patrick away from home engaged in his medical studies and Hugh on the high seas fulfilling his dreams of becoming an officer in the merchant navy, Tom had been left without a male hand to restrain him. In one letter to his mother, Hugh refers to the lad 'running wild about the farm'. After Hugh's death Jessie had been too busy running the farm to pay close attention to what her two youngest children were doing and Tom and Lizzie seem to have been given a much looser rein during their upbringing than their older siblings. Patrick quite clearly considered that he had a special responsibility to see that the youngest members of the family, orphaned at such an early age that they had never known a father's discipline, should want for nothing. His younger sister, Lizzie, unlike Janet, was encouraged to become a scholar at a time when education for girls was considered almost indecent. Patrick paid for her education at the college in Edinburgh for the Daughters of Ministers and Gentlemen (the school which Mary MacIntyre had also attended) out of his own pocket. Since Tom showed no inclination towards an academic career however, Patrick assumed his young brother would follow John and work on the farm. This, Tom did grudgingly having never been consulted about his future. In John's absence he assumed a pseudo-managerial role on the farm, ordering the men about in an inappropriate manner for such a

Luing was the larder of the Slate Islands. Her fertile valleys provided most of the meal and much of the meat, milk and dairy products demanded by the very large quarrying population. In the 1790s Breadalbane decrofted the island, requiring his former crofters to become employees of the Factor. Although a few of the younger elements emigrated rather than work for another, most of the agricultural workers accepted the change. All the fertile land became one model farm centered on the house of Breadalbane's tacksman at Ardlarach, near Toberonochy. The cow byre was sufficiently large to keep all the cattle under cover during the harsh winter months thus relieving the proprietor of the necessity of disposing of almost all his stock to the drovers in the latter part of the year. There were several grain mills both on Luing and Seil but this at Achafolla, close to the medieval chapel of Kilchattan and the Achafolla Public School, continued working well into the twentieth century.

young boy. Jessie, although fearful that her staff might take umbrage and depart leaving her single-handed, appears to have done little to curb his high spirits.

Tom, perhaps not recognising the amount of work and dedication to duty which had brought it about, appears to have resented always the success of his older siblings in their various enterprises. Although Lizzie had had no more encouragement than he in applying herself to her studies, Tom was most envious of the attention which Patrick paid to her. He clearly considered himself to have been at the back of the queue when the benefits were being handed out.

When John eventually returned from his adventures overseas and began to take some responsibility for the farm, Tom, although still little more than a schoolboy, made it clear that he considered his position as farm manager had been usurped. It seems that as the years passed this resentment never abated despite the fact that in order to appease their mother the two brothers continued to work Dunmore Farm together until her death.

Not everyone in the district was respectful of the family at Dunmore. There were those who held a grudge, like the neighbouring farmer, a Mr Campbell, who was the tenant of the adjoining estate of Ardencaple. Without any supporting evidence, Campbell accused Patrick's dog of worrying his sheep and rather than make an official complaint either to Patrick himself or to the police, he put it about the village that the doctor's dog had done the damage. Patrick wrote to him to set him right:

Easdale                                                                October 22nd 1894

Dear Mr Campbell

I am very sorry to hear of the worrying which has occurred among your sheep and hope you will get some compensation for your loss. It is a pity more care was not taken in identifying the dog as it is a perfect impossibility for my dog to have been on your farm on the nights you mention. I am the more positive of this as on both those nights I was away from home and took the trouble to lock up the dog in case he would follow me. He was not released until between seven and eight next morning. Indeed it is on a very rare occasion that he is let out at night at all unless to accompany myself so that your suspicion is absolutely without foundation. This is the more to be regretted as it seems to me as wicked to miscall a dog as to defame a man. I hope however that for your own sake and the sake of neighbouring farmers that you will see the policeman about it or else take proper means to discover the offender.

I am, yours sincerely,

Patrick H Gillies

In complete contrast to Mr Campbell, Jessie was quick to make amends when she learned the truth about injury to one of her cows. On finding the cow had wandered because a gate was left open and had subsequently been fatally injured she overreacted by calling the local constable. There had been a spate of vandalism in the village recently and she was convinced that this was another example. When the Law had completed its investigations however it turned out that the offender was a young boy well known to the Gillies family. The offence was now deemed to be accidental rather than an act of vandalism and, full of remorse, Jessie at once wrote to the chief constable withdrawing her accusation.

When Janet (Jessie) Hunter Gillies died in 1896 she left John and Thomas in charge of the farm at Dunmore. As neither of the men was any hand at figures, Patrick took over his mother's clerical duties associated with the farm and his letter book contains as much correspondence related to this as to his medical practice. Jessie's death gave John the opportunity he had been looking for to obtain a place of his own where he need no longer be in constant conflict with his brother Tom. With the small legacy left to him by his mother and with Patrick's help, he took a lease on the Clachan farm on the mainland side of the Clachan Bridge. John never married and was always a solitary figure. He spent the remaining ten years of his life alone but for occasional visits from his brother Pat and his young nephews.

In 1905, possibly in order to clear up any remaining disagreement between the brothers, John and Thomas agreed to a valuation being carried out at Dunmore farm. The details, listed in Patrick's letter book, show that the farm was valued at a little over £3,000 which included ten cows and a shorthorn bull, twelve store cattle and seven calves. There were in addition more than three hundred ewes, seven rams of champion quality and sixty hogs. Seventy-six acres were under crops consisting mainly of animal feed, although four acres were under potatoes and nine were planted with turnips. The farm produce was valued at one hundred and sixty pounds.

When he died in 1907, John Gillies' estate, including the lease on the Clachan farm, was left to be divided amongst his siblings. The amount was not inconsiderable for John appears to have saved money made during his time abroad and each of the Gillieses received a sum of around one hundred and fifty pounds. Immediately following his brother's death, Patrick found a buyer for the lease on the Clachan farm but this gentleman stayed only a few months before changing his mind in favour of a smallholding on the Isle of Skye. With three years of the lease remaining, it was agreed amongst the family members that Tom should

*The short haymaking season necessitated the building of small ricks which allowed the hay to dry out more quickly. These pudding-like structures so much more picturesque than today's black plastic silage bags, were peculiar to Scotland.*

take it on and with Patrick's financial assistance he bought what remained of the lease from John's estate.

Until now, Patrick had assigned the lease of Dunmore House to his mother and, upon her death, to his brothers, taking the lease on Ballachuan for Mary and himself. With John now dead and Tom away to Clachan Farm, he sublet Ballachuan House and moved with his wife and family into Dunmore House. He retained the lease on Ballachuan, however, in order to ensure the availability of a residence suitable for any locum doctor he might be obliged to engage in the future.

Once Patrick and his family were installed in Dunmore House the doctor took a greater hand in the physical work on the farm and in his diary of 1911 he mentions a number of occasions when he helped with the planting of turnips, the lambing and the repairing of fences. With Tom now running his own farm at Clachan, it was left to Patrick to administer Dunmore. This he managed with the help of two permanent farmworkers and casual assistance from the sub-tenant of Cairnban. Unlike her mother-in-law, Mary Gillies was not skilled in cheese and butter making but she did manage to oversee the work of a couple of female servants who continued to run the dairy. The farm went on supplying milk and dairy products to the district until Patrick finally relinquished the lease in 1919; this despite the fact that the doctor removed his family to Connel in 1914, leaving a manager in charge of the farm and giving it only cursory supervision himself.

Thomas Gillies, finding himself at last in a position where he might prove himself by his own decisions and activity, managed the Clachan farm for the next seven years with some degree of success. In the three years prior to the First World War, however, there was another period of great depression in the slate industry and Tom, whose income depended upon his supplying the slate quarries with fodder for the horses as well as providing grain for the quarry villages, began to experience financial problems.

With the exception of the quarries at Cullipool and Dalvica, all were now closed down for several months in every year. Families began to drift away to find work elsewhere, many emigrating to Canada and the Antipodes. Depleted of its young folks, and left with an aging population unable to work, the Slate Islands experienced their worst crisis in a long history of success and failure. The problem this time was relieved only by the declaration of war in August 1914.

With the outbreak of war, small armaments factories sprung up providing work for ex-quarrymen with engineering skills. The Clyde shipyards were demanding labour and opened their arms to the skilled engineers of Argyll. Those who joined the armed services were able to send home money to sustain their families. Young men, who had emigrated only a year or two before, returned to join up and were again able to support their parents and other dependents. For the farming community this change was particularly welcome. Suddenly there was a demand for meat and wool. The population as a whole became more affluent and housewives were able to demand the more expensive dairy products sold by Dunmore Farm.

For Tom Gillies however, relief came almost too late. Although he had run the farm at Clachan in a conscientious manner for some years, the combination of local depression in the market and the tardy manner in which several of his creditors paid their bills had placed him in dire straights. Just at a time when he was preparing to go off to the war, Patrick found himself having to intervene to save his brother from bankruptcy or even worse.

With his brother's assistance, Thomas Gillies survived the threat of bankruptcy and lived on in the district until his death on 14 Nov 1935, four years after Patrick himself. He was buried beside his brothers in the Kilbrandon kirkyard.

As it had been in the early days, Dunmore House was again let to holidaymakers for the summer months, the rent making a welcome addition to the income of the estate. Although by 1914 Patrick was spending much of his time at his new house in Connel, he appeared loath to relinquish control of what everyone regarded as the family home presumably because one of his boys, at least two of whom seemed destined for a career in medicine, might wish to inherit the Easdale Practice. With this in mind, when agreeing to his new appointment with Argyll County Council Patrick had made the proviso that he should continue to treat his private patients in the parish of Kilbrandon and Kilchattan. Just as Jessie had done for him, he wished to ensure that there would still be a medical practice for one of his sons to take over when qualified.

Patrick's hopes in this respect were to be dashed however when in 1914 personal tragedy followed almost at once by the outbreak of war, swept away many of his dreams for the future. Left bereft and dejected, he became indifferent to the future of both the farm and the medical practice and was to spend the war years and their aftermath struggling to rid himself of all responsibility for both.

Relinquishing the farm proved more difficult than he could have thought possible. During wartime there were requirements upon the farming community to contribute as much as possible to vital food supplies. It was essential that there should be no period of winding down or any interference with the maximum productivity of the farm. Buying and selling of land leases was held very much in abeyance as many of those who might have been interested in making a purchase were otherwise engaged at the battle front. Despite his rejection of Dunmore, Patrick found himself obliged to continue to manage its affairs and from 1915 onwards he entered into a protracted correspondence with Breadalbane's factor regarding the subleasing of Dunmore farm. In a letter of August 1915, when he was already enroute to the Middle East as a captain in the Royal Army Medical Corps, he wrote determining the number of sheep to be kept by the tenant, while as late as 1919 he was writing to Breadalbane's agent from Inverness, where he was stationed while working for the ministry of pensions.

18th April 1919

[. . .] There is a question of improvements under this submission. These are;

1. The laying down to permanent pasture of 20 acres. The exact acreage and compensation to be determined by the valuators
2. Unexhausted values of
   a) Oats and other feeding stuff consumed on farm
   b) Bought-in feeding stuffs
   c) Artificial manure

I think these are all...With regard to repairs the points I would ask laid down are that

1. Repairs that are called 'landlord's' are not to include those which Landlord already refused to execute.
2. That the standard of repair is the condition as it existed in 1915.
3. That apart from ordinary deficiencies I am the judge of repairs necessary.
4. That renewals are not included as repairs. For instance a door may be repaired but not renewed.
5. That I do not consider there are any repairs or deficiencies at my outgoing. (This is at your own suggestion)
6. Anything further you think competent.

Yours faithfully,

Patrick H Gillies

There was obvious relief when in 1919 Patrick was able to record in his diary that the leases upon both Ballahuan and Dunmore had at last been relinquished.

# 7 An African Interlude

$P$ATRICK GILLIES HAD, ever since his first experience of the power wielded by the Local Authority, been attracted to the idea of a public service role where he might exercise the organisational and administrative abilities which he possessed. His first attempt to obtain a post in such administration was made in 1900 only three years after gaining his degree in Public Health and Sanitary Engineering. The post of Chief Medical Officer of Health for the County of Sutherland was advertised and Patrick made his application supported by a number of glowing references from his tutors both at Edinburgh and Glasgow Universities and from the superintendents of those hospitals in the north of England where he had worked for a short time before coming to Easdale.

At twenty-eight years of age he might well be considered somewhat presumptuous in applying for a post of this rank. The chief medical officers appointed by county councils normally found promotion through the ranks of public administration and reached the pinnacle almost as a sinecure for long and faithful service. Patrick, however, although young, believed himself to be sufficiently experienced and well-qualified for the post and, what was perhaps more important, he had the necessary youth and vigour to carry out the reforms in the public heath service which he considered long overdue. While his application was considered politely and afforded the compliment of an interview with members of Sutherland County Council, he was outvoted on the grounds that another more senior medical person, who had been long in the employ of the authority, was more deserving. He returned to his various activities at Easdale, disappointed but determined to find a way by a different route. He decided to concentrate on another idea which had been forming in his mind ever since he joined the school board. His plan, concerning the regular medical examination of school children throughout the county, was one of immense proportions involving considerable research before he could put it into the form of an official paper for consideration by the county council. Before he could even begin the work, however, a much more pressing engagement awaited him.

Among Patrick's many interests within the parish was his membership of the 1st Argyll (Easdale) Artillery Company of the Volunteers, forerunner of the Territorials, founded in 1907, and the present Territorial Army. Acting as the company's medical officer and performing additional duties such as those of company clerk and treasurer, he attended weekly parades and accompanied the men to camp every year. His role was almost unique, few Volunteer companies being able to claim to have their own surgeon. When in 1901 the conflict with the Boer farmers in South Africa became hopelessly bogged down the Volunteers were called upon to supply a battalion of troops to augment the depleted regular British Army. Little is recorded about the men who joined the Volunteers' battalion in South Africa except that eight of them came from Argyll and Bute companies, and because Patrick was one of very few surgeons to serve in the Volunteers he was invited to accompany them.

One wonders how Mary Gillies reacted to the news that she was to be left with two small children, one an infant of a few months, and a medical practice operated by a locum doctor to supervise while her husband went off to war. For Patrick it was an exciting new adventure. Since being refused the post he had sought, he had been restless and irritable, finding fault with his fellow parish councillors and Local Authority officials alike. It may be his wife was quite relieved to see him go while they still had a few friends left. It was, after all, to be for a short while only. The Scottish contingent of the Volunteers reported to Fort George on the Moray Firth for an initial period of training before taking ship for the Cape. Shortly after his arrival at Cape Town in the spring of 1901, Patrick was posted as medical officer in charge of a military hospital in the Natal province.

No one had expected a bunch of Dutch farmers untrained in the arts of war to be able to hold out for any length of time against the superior might of the British Army. The Dutchmen were, however, fighting on home ground and seemed able to launch devastating attacks out of nowhere and then fade into the landscape at will. It didn't help of course that the British soldier was still wearing the traditional red uniform which stood out for miles in that sparse bush country. Only when the British themselves adopted similar tactics to those of the enemy, attacking by stealth, often behind enemy lines, and dressing their troops in khaki instead of red tunics, did they begin to make inroads into the Boer's territory. The casualties inflicted upon the British by the Boers were formidable and Patrick was immediately confronted with every kind of battle wound as well as illnesses such as malaria and sleeping sickness and over exposure to the hot African sun.

At this date little progress had yet been made towards the well-coordinated, fully equipped Royal Army Medical Corps (RAMC) we know today. Patrick would have found himself in charge of a tented city staffed in the main by inexperienced young doctors but, with luck, also a few nursing sisters. Unfortunately the climate was considered unsuitable for women and few of them stayed long enough to form a cohesive team. Patrick was lucky to have joined the service some three years after the RAMC became recognised as an official corps of the military but it was still regarded by many commanding officers as an encumbrance to be endured rather than welcomed. Surgeons were treated as inferior members of staff and the instructions issued by senior medical personnel were often disregarded.

At the start of the campaign in Egypt and the Sudan there had been very few medical facilities, staffed only by civilian doctors on short-term contracts. There was little coordination of the activities of these medical men and the piecemeal arrangements did little to encourage the kind of research which might have improved the medical services provided on the battlefield.

When Patrick arrived in Africa in 1901 the RAMC, at just three years old, was still very far from being prepared for expansion to meet the needs of a fighting force which was by now scattered over much of southern Africa. Yet the medical planning was, or so it seemed before the crunch, on quite a substantial scale. Eight hundred and fifty doctors had been despatched to the various areas of operation, backed by ten hospitals. As the conflict spread, and heavy casualties from ill-judged frontal assaults began to occur, the size of the armed forces had to be trebled. By the end of the war, three years later, the numbers in the Medical Corps had reached eight-and-a-half thousand, and there were twenty-one thousand hospital beds available. These were, like the fighting, scattered over half the continent.

For a man of compassion, as Patrick Gillies clearly was, it must have come as a great shock on his arrival in Africa to encounter the insensitivity of those of his colleagues who were already well versed in traditional army medical practices. Patrick had entered the profession at a time when asepsis was generally accepted in civilian practice and where anaesthesia was no longer a mere gimmick to be administered to the fairer sex during childbirth but scorned by virile, stoic man. While Patrick was aware of the incredible ability of the human to endure extremes both of pain and hardship he had been trained to carry out surgery using anaesthetics, when the work could be undertaken with greater care. He was no stranger to surgery without anaesthesia, however, and even if he himself had never had to practice it, he had been brought up on the tales told of heroic operations to sever limbs or remove tumours in record-breaking times! Much of the seeming barbarity of medical care before Simpson's discovery of chloroform in 1846, and for many decades after, had been due to the total absence of any kind of anaesthetic. In the Easdale medical practice during the 1860s and 1870s amputations and other operations had been carried out without benefit of anaesthetic and painful surgery was still within the living memory of all. Sadly, during the South African campaign the Regular Army surgeons saw the use of chloroform as an unnecessary refinement, lacking the benefit of any form of pain relief other than alcohol, soldiers were expected to clamp down on a leather strap and bear the three or four minutes it took to sever a limb or remove a bullet with fortitude and without a murmur. On his arrival at his field hospital Patrick must have been appalled to find that such methods still existed and, what was worse, that many amputations might have been avoided altogether had greater care been taken to avoid sepsis in the first place!

With so many patients requiring attention he could hardly criticise too roundly the medical officer who doled out 'Number 9s', a purgative of heroic calibre, for every ailment presented. Nor could he condemn out of hand the practice of putting 'Medicine and Duty', written in red ink on the reports of those suspected of malingering. After all, these older surgeons were only following a pattern laid down by centuries of experience of war. He could, however, bring some order into the exercise of the day-to-day duties of the medical staff in his own hospital and teach them by his own example the basic rules of hygiene and aseptic surgical practice.

From the twenty-first-century comfort of a clinically clean hospital administering tried and tested drugs with the benefit of the X-ray and the electron microscope for diagnosis, it is easy for us to condemn the nineteenth-century army surgeon for his callous treatment of the men in his care. Like every other officer, however, the military surgeon's first duty was to get men back into the line as fast as possible and many of his patients would prefer to grin and bear their ailments rather than subject themselves to the medical officer's treatment! If Patrick wished to resist the Army's well-established procedures, and there is little doubt that he did, he would have to tread carefully and inaugurate changes by stealth. He certainly had the courage and compassion to make such changes as his later record during his service with the Army pensions boards will show.

While the powers that be in the War Office fought their beaurocratic battles, surgeons in the field like Patrick battled with more than one enemy. As always, transport for the wounded was a prime difficulty and a journey for a badly hurt man in an ox wagon, without springs, must have been almost unendurable; it was also seriously damaging, if not lethal. After a short stay in the front-line dressing station the wounded often faced a long train journey in crudely fitted out-cattle trucks. The men received in Patrick's hospital fell into this category and he must frequently have witnessed cases where greater speed and more careful handling would have saved a life. Added to this, the liaison between the bearer companies and the field hospitals was poor. Bearers were attached to a parent unit of fighting men. They left the battlefield only to carry the wounded and having delivered their casualty they returned to their battalion. It took a long series of negotiations to persuade Army personnel that the bearers should be attached to the field hospital and remain in the hospital for orderly duties when the battle was over!

The main enemy was not the resourceful Boer, with his modern Mauser rifle and expert marksmanship. The typhoid bacillus soon became the chief killer and the incidence of sick men far outstripped the wounded. Standards of hygiene in the Army were still poor. Field-Marshal Lord Wolseley, commander-in-chief of the British Army took the view that the sanitation officer was the most use-less person in the Army, who could well be left behind at base. The general attitude is best summed up in an unofficial extract from a royal commission on this war, 'Regarding hygiene and sanitation, Tommy doesn't understand it, and his officer regards it as just a fad.' Simple precautions such as boiling all drinking water were often neglected, and the epidemic of bowel infections rose to a total of a hundred thousand patients. Here, Patrick's experience was brought to the fore. While he had no jurisdiction over the conduct of food preparation, waste disposal and living conditions generally at the front, he was in charge of these matters in his own medical facility. His application of rigorous conditions in matters of sanitation and personal hygiene, regular inspection of food preparation areas and insistence upon the greatest care in using aseptic methods in the treatment of wounds must have made a substantial difference.

Although it was possible at this time to inoculate the troops against the typhoid bacillus there was a great deal of resistance to this form of preventative medicine. For certain, the anti-bacterial serum was not 100 per cent effective, but the truth was that the brave British soldier was frightened of the needle and seized upon any excuse to avoid it! When rumours were spread that inoculations against typhoid impaired virility, this was sufficient to invoke a rebellion against all inoculations. Only fourteen thosuand men were given anti-typhoid inoculations in this war and among these the incidence of typhoid was scarcely halved. The Army, reacting without recourse to its own medical experts, compounded the quite unfounded rumours of infertility by restricting typhoid vaccination to volunteers who were unmarried. The final score in the rival claims of typhoid and Boer bullets was fourteen thousand dead from disease and six thousand killed in action, while those discharged sick from fever greatly outnumbered the wounded.

For the gunshot wounds encountered during the conflict prognosis for recovery was relatively favourable. The newer type of high-velocity bullet with a hard nose made a far less damaging wound than outdated weapons such as the cannon ball. Most importantly, the ammunition was cleaner and the risk of primary infection very much reduced. The soil over which battles with the Boers were fought was generally dry and sandy, not riddled with the deadly organisms which were later found in Flanders mud; there was little risk of either tetanus or the deadly infection known as 'gas gangrene'.

Improvements in both the number and quality of surgeons recruited and the facilities in which they practised led to better records being kept and to some exceptional research into the treatment of battle wounds. Surgeons working on the Veld were not deterred from tackling a gunshot wound to the head with a depressed compound fracture of the skull. It was recognised that such injuries were a clear indication for surgery in order to remove bone fragments pressing on the brain. There was also some success in dealing with penetrating wounds of the chest. More than 70 per cent of these men recovered. There is little doubt that Patrick's skills as a surgeon, honed as they had been by similar injuries encountered in the slate quarries, were brought to the fore during this period.

Inadvertently, Patrick Gillies had been preparing in more ways than one for his tour of duty in Africa during the ten years he had already spent at Easdale. One aspect of his work was created by Lord Kitchener himself: Patrick may well have been responsible for the care not only of wounded soldiers but also of civilians placed in one of those disastrous detention camps organised by Kitchener and his staff for the 'protection' of Boer women and children. The Boers were unused to close communal life, and their personal habits were none too particular. A small family living in wild country perhaps forty or fifty miles from the nearest neighbour had no use for even the most primitive sanitary facilities. A communal privy was foreign to those used to squatting in the bush when need arose. In the forty-six so-called 'concentration camps' there were a total of twenty thousand deaths among their hundred and seventeen thousand inmates. Kitchener never went near any of his internment camps but this did not deter him from reporting to Lord Roberts that the camps were 'very well run'. It was only the dispatches from members of the British press, including Winston Churchill, which drew attention to the true state of affairs. RAMC staff were presented with an added burden of responsibility that might well have been avoided and it was left to the initiative of surgeons such as Patrick Gillies, already experienced in the control of disease in overcrowded communities, to cope with the outcome.

Many historians have chosen to criticise the conduct of the South African campaign and in particular the medical attention given to troops and civilians alike. For the individual medical officer, however, there can be nothing but praise. Faced with an epidemic of typhoid, with no cure, and with an average mortality of about 10 per cent he had to rely entirely upon his own initiative. To compound his difficulties his field hospital was most probably sited near the shallow trench latrines of previous troops on the march or perhaps on ground formerly occupied by the Boers. In addition to disease, he had to cope with sunstroke and heatstroke, conditions not then understood. Plagued with flies that spread dysentery, but without any of the modern deterrents, he was expected during a battle to go forward and recover the wounded under fire. As that brave and generous commander, Sir Ian Hamilton, asserted, 'Nothing could surpass the devotion either of doctors or the nursing sisters with whom I had contact. The charge of unpreparedness may stick, but no shortcomings could conceal what the men of the (Medical) Corps achieved by sheer endurance and fortitude.' No one was more exposed to the risk of disease than the nursing sisters, orderlies and doctors in these improvised hospitals where they were constantly surrounded by highly infectious patients and contaminated material of all kinds. Three hundred members of the Medical Corps paid with their lives for this form of devotion, while their awards for gallantry on the field of battle were on a scale only surpassed by the Royal Artillery. Among these there were six Victoria Crosses.

In 1901 the shortage of surgeons was critical. The arrangements to rectify this were hasty and entirely inadequate. One leading surgeon who had been persuaded to lend his services for a while, described the situation as impossible. He later talked of 'the exigencies of a slowly-grown, iron-bound system, clogged with petty trivialities, and hampered at every turn'.★ We have already seen how Patrick Gillies responded to intractable beaurocracy in his dealings with Argyll County Council. His response to obsolete and inappropriate Army regulations could have been no different, but whereas the distinguished but disillusioned surgeon noted above hurriedly left the field, Patrick saw out his contract to the bitter end. He returned to Easdale in the autumn of 1901 an older and wiser man, with a wealth of experience which was to see him in good stead fourteen years later, at Gallipoli.

★ Redmond McLaughlan, *The Royal Army Medical Corps* (London, 1972).

# 8 The Next Generation

B<small>Y THE SUMMER</small> of 1902 the doctor was back in the Slate Islands, carrying out his normal duties in his Slate Island parish. He arrived home to find his wife delivered of their third child, Hugh. Hunter was now a lively little four year old, already learning to read and write under his mother's instruction, while Alexander Cameron (Cammie) showed every sign of being just as smart as his older brother. The Gillieses were to have just one more child, John, generally known as Jackie, who was born in 1908, six years after Hugh. With the isolation hospital up and running Patrick could turn his attention to his family and the more weighty aspects of his daily encounters with parish life.

Ballachuan House was some distance from any school. It was a walk of nearly three miles from Ballachuan House to Easdale Public School, even taking the short cut across the hill behind the church and past the ancient hill-fort of Cnoc an Tighe Mhoir and on to Smiddy Brae. Although distances covered on foot were far greater than they are today, Mary considered the school too far away for her little boys. As infants the doctor's children were taught at home by their mother. What better teacher could they have had than one who had taught the daughters of the rich and famous in Edinburgh?

Patrick, however, did not consider this form of education suitable for two growing boys and when Hunter was seven years of age and Cammie five, they were enrolled in the village school at Easdale. Every day Hunter and his wee brother would set off on the two-mile trek, taking the short cut over Smiddy Brae and down to the shore past their uncles' home at Dunmore. Today it seems

*Ballachuan House, near Cuan, was taken over by Patrick and Mary soon after their marriage and was the birthplace of their four sons.*

hardly conceivable that such young children might be allowed to travel so far alone but it has to be remembered that this was a parish in which the population, although widespread, was in close communication. The doctor's boys were well known and their activities would be noted as they passed the various dwellings on their way. From the point of view of molestation it was as safe as anywhere, and as for the dangers of the natural environment these had been firmly instilled in the minds of the two boys since earliest childhood. Having been raised on the folklore of the district by their nursemaid they were only too aware of bogs where a man and his horse might be swallowed up and lost without trace and they avoided the sheer cliffs from where an erstwhile local hero had rained down arrows upon marauding Vikings as they attempted to sail through Easdale Sound.

There was always plenty to engage the attention of the young lads on these daily journeys: wildlife to observe, rocks to examine, old ruins to explore. While the boys were in no apparent danger there were plenty of opportunities for them to get into mischief, but it was all a part of growing up and getting to know the world about them. For the most part their father looked tolerably upon their misdemeanours although their mother may have been a little more severe when need arose.

Both Hunter and Cammie applied themselves diligently to their lessons and early showed that they had it in them to become the doctors that Patrick wanted them to be. Hunter was a pale, rather aesthetic character more interested in his books than the rough and tumble of the school yard. The only athletic exercise he was ever to indulge in was long-distance running for which he claimed some success at his Edinburgh school. Cammie on the other hand, although no slouch at his lessons, involved himself in every sporting activity that presented itself. He could handle a ball with the greatest proficiency, whatever its size

*Alexander (Cammie), Hugh and Jackie Gillies with a friend c.1916*

or shape and was to become as well known for his prowess on the golf course as on the rugby field. There is little doubt that both the boys benefited from those early morning scampers over the hills to school.

At the village school Hunter and Cammie applied themselves to their work in scholarly fashion studying the normal curriculum of reading, writing and arithmetic enhanced by more advanced studies in science, geography and applied mathematics. In addition, they received coaching in the classics from Patrick's friend Sam MacDougall and became proficient in both Latin and Greek.

Having been deprived in their infant days of the company of the more rumbustious village children, both Hunter and Cammie might have been in danger of becoming milk sops or mummy's darlings had Patrick not taken a hand in their outdoor activities. Even as very young children, the boys were expected to accompany their father on long walks and to help him to sail the small boat which he used for getting about in his island-strewn practice. From the family retainer, a fellow who took care of Patrick's horses and sailed the boat when necessary, they learned to fish, and in his company they encountered the local fishermen and the quarrymen who gathered on the piers when a steamer was due, or around the doors of the Tigh an Truish Inn of a summer evening. Here the men would meet for a smoke and a chat, their conversations rich in reminiscence and adventure sufficient to capture the imagination of the young Gillieses.

At eleven years both Hunter and Cammie were sent to George Watson's Academy in Edinburgh. Hunter, always more taken up with his books than events on the playing field, shone in his lessons but never excelled in sport. At the Easdale school Cammie had excelled in soccer but at Watson's Academy he discovered a talent for handling a rugby football and soon found himself among the first to be picked for either game. Although no slouch in the classroom, Cammie was to become a leading player in the school's teams at every level of his school career, finally playing for Watsonian Old Boys when he had hardly left school. The culmination of his footballing career came when in 1928 he was selected to play for Scotland. Having enlisted for a short while in the Royal Artillery in 1918, Cammie completed his medical studies in Edinburgh and after a period as houseman in the Royal Infirmary and six months at the Cumberland Hospital in Carlisle took a partnership in a medical practice in Macclesfield, Lancashire, where he was to remain for the rest of his working life. He married Mary Irene Carr and with her had two children, Patrick and Fiona.

*Cammie on his graduation from Edinburgh University at the age of twenty five in 1925.*

*Scotland v. England at Twickenham 1935. Cammie is presented to King George V.*

*Rugby football international, Cammie, or Sandy Gillies as he was known in Rugby Union circles, was noted for his prodigious kicking. During his career he kicked in excess of five hundred goals for his club, Watsonians. Selected to join the British Lions Tour of South Africa in the 1930s he was obliged to decline because he could not leave his medical practice in Macclesfield.*

Hugh, Patrick and Mary's third child, promised to be as bright as his brothers and progressed quite as satisfactorily with his school work until, at the age of nine years, he met with a serious accident which nearly cost him his life. Travelling from Glasgow to Oban on the Oban and Callander Railway in July 1911 Hugh was accompanied by his mother, Mary's sister, Mrs Smith and his young brother, Jackie. The afternoon was hot and the journey long and tedious and, like any young boy, Hugh, having quickly tired of the books his mother had brought along to entertain him, looked about for something more interesting to do. Claiming that it was too hot, he insisted upon releasing the leather strap which secured the window and lowered it to its full extent. It is unlikely that he intended to unlock the door but one must suppose that while leaning out of the window to catch a breath of air he fiddled with the outside fittings and unintentionally depressed the door handle so that the door flew open, slamming back against the side of the carriage. Before either of the ladies was able to make a move, the boy had been pulled out through the door opening and had fallen onto the track. It was only by good fortune that he fell between the rails and out of the way of wheels on the following coaches. The two distraught women screamed and shouted to no avail. There was no corridor on the train and this was before the days when all carriages were fitted by law with an automatic device for stopping the train in an emergency. One can imagine the sheer terror of the mother

*Patrick's son Hugh aged 5, 1907.*

and her sister as they waited impatiently for the train to cover the remaining three miles from the Pass of Brander to the next stop at Taynuilt station, a matter of some ten minutes. It was as much as Mrs Smith could do to prevent her sister from dropping down onto the track herself, to run back to the aid of her child. The 29 July 1911 issue of the *Oban Times* carried the following report, which lacked something in accuracy:

### Report of Accident to Jackie Gillies Aged 3 years.

It was with deep regret that the news was received here on Saturday evening that the youngest child of Dr P H Gillies, Dunmore, had that day accidentally fallen on the line from a railway carriage in which his mother, her sister, Mrs Smith, and other members of their family were travelling from Glasgow to Oban. Efforts were made to have the train stopped but the attention of the guard could not be directed to the fact. The train continued on its journey to Taynuilt before the alarm could be given. The mishap took place in the Pass of Brander. Meantime the officials of a goods train noticed the little fellow lying unconscious on the line. They immediately proceeded with him to Taynuilt where he was put under medical treatment. He remained unconscious until Monday. He is recovering somewhat and there are happily prospects of a speedy recovery.

Hugh was of course considerably older than reported by the *Oban Times* the reporter having confused the victim with his younger brother, Jackie.

The two women did not have long to wait at Taynuilt. The article is correct in its report that Hugh was picked up by another train. At Taynuilt station the sorry little casualty was unloaded from the coal tender, there being no carriage on a goods train. Medical attention in the shape of the local doctor was quickly sought and word sent by telegraph to Patrick at Ballachuan. Young Hugh remained unconscious for more than forty-eight hours and Patrick feared he might never recover. Children are very resilient, however, and within days the boy was running about as though nothing had happened.

It was a while before Mary began to notice the difference the accident had made to her son. At first she told herself that his sudden loss of concentration and his apparent inability to learn new things was a passing phase which would be overcome as he grew older. His short-term memory never completely recovered however and it was necessary for him to be told repeatedly if something required to be done. Fortunately for young Hughie his schooling was still in the care of his mother whose infinite patience helped him to progress, slowly but steadily. Had he been subjected to the rigours of an ordinary classroom it is

unlikely he would have achieved any learning whatsoever. Patrick found it very hard to accept that a son of his would not be a scholar. Throughout the boy's childhood he tried to force learning into him, albeit in a kindly rather than a brutal manner. But, try as he would to please his father, Hugh just could not remember all those facts, the

*Patrick's son Hugh aged 19, c.1921*

dates, names and events required of growing boys in the classroom. Not able to accept defeat, Patrick nevertheless enrolled the boy at Watson's Academy with his brothers. Hugh appears to have found some solace in learning to play the bagpipes and photographs exist of him kitted out as a piper in the school's military band. Although Hugh was innately just as intelligent as his brothers he became easily flustered and was unable to function under pressure. Eventually he found the ideal occupation in a job which was much envied by many young men of the day: he became a trainee cinema projectionist. His open, sunny personality stood him in good stead and eventually he was promoted to manager and at the age of twenty-eight took charge of the cinema in Holyhead, Anglesea. There followed a number of management posts in cinemas in North Wales before his appointment to Welshpool where he remained until his retirement. Here he became a well-known and respected member of the community, remembered for his quietly spoken manner, his great sense of humour and the friendly way in which he greeted all his customers. His staff, meanwhile, appreciated his benevolent, open-door policy in his dealings with them. Hugh married and had two daughters, Patricia and Davinia.

Patrick and Mary's youngest son, Jackie, was certainly no slouch at his lessons. He followed his brothers to Watson's Academy where he studied for the Ministry, but much to Patrick's chagrin he failed to gain admission to theological college due to a weakness in classical subjects. He was happy enough, however, to work hard at his mathematics which lead him on to studies in engineering and navigation. Jackie had inherited from his uncle Hugh a taste for the salt sea. As a boy he devoted every spare moment to sailing and if he could not be on the sea he was reading about it or mingling on the dock with the old sea-salts who had returned to the islands in their retirement. When he had completed his studies satisfactorily, at the age of seventeen in the year 1925, he was apprenticed to a mercantile shipping company. Rising to the rank of purser, he remained with the company until 1945. Having completed a number of Atlantic crossings in U-Boat infested waters, he found himself stranded for some months aboard ship in harbour in Baltimore, USA. The ship remained in dock long enough for Jackie to meet and marry his American-born wife, Alma. The ship finally sailed for Liverpool late in 1945. Halfway across the Atlantic, Jackie died of a heart attack. He was thirty-seven years of age. His body was brought back to Scotland and lies in the family plot in the Kilbrandon cemetery.

*Midshipman Jackie Gillies with his skipper aboard ship, c.1930.*

Most poignant of all these stories of Patrick's family is that of his eldest son, Hunter. In 1913 the two older boys were settled in at Watson's Academy and well on their way to careers in medicine. With Hugh being prepared for acceptance into Watson's despite his early setback, and Jackie showing every sign of being as academically able as his eldest brothers, Patrick, able at last to take up his new post with the Local Authority, might well have been counting his blessings. However, Fate was to test him more severely than he could have imagined in any of his wildest nightmares.

*Patrick's son Hunter shortly before his death at age 16 in 1914.*

In the latter part of 1913, when the family was considering quitting Dunmore for good and taking up residence at Connel, Hunter became ill. He developed a chest cold which prevented him returning to school for the autumn term. The chest condition did not clear up as it should and although reluctant to admit to anything worse than a mild infection, Patrick nevertheless decided it would be in the boy's best interest to stay at Dunmore. The move was delayed again when after Christmas Hunter still showed no sign of improvement. As the summer of 1914 approached, Patrick began to fear the worst. He called in specialist friends who confirmed his diagnosis that the boy was suffering from a particularly virulent form of pulmonary tuberculosis. Both parents were at last forced to accept that their son was dying.

At this time there was no cure for the dreaded disease. The only way to combat it was to expose the patient to plenty of fresh air and good nourishing food. If the frame was strong enough and the patient's will to live great enough, there might be some hope of prolonging life, but not indefinitely. Ironically, in December 1912, Patrick had been asked to submit a report on a proposal by the county medical officer, Dr McNeill, to provide temporary shelters for phthisical patients (the term tuberculosis or TB was not yet commonly in use). Patrick's response included the following observations:

> For suitable cases there can be no question that such shelters or bedrooms would be of great value in treatment and isolation. Unfortunately consumption, although not a frequent disease in this parish, occurs generally among those who in the present state of affairs can get plenty of fresh air but cannot obtain an adequate supply of the poorest fare … When by and by, the parties fully appreciate the infectious nature of Tubercular Disease and the importance of such methods as the Local Authorities are adopting towards suppression, even eradication of the disease, they, the people themselves, will become protagonists in the struggle. In the meantime while there remains a firm belief in the hereditary transmission, realisation of the infectivity of Consumption is vague.

Patrick went on to stress the importance of educating the people and in particular the school children, in all aspects of the disease. He concluded his report as follows:

> The question of the expense of administration will undoubtedly be a great consideration where the powers of taxation are limited, but this must already have been considered in the proposed conversion of Dalmally hospital for the same purpose. In any case will not Argyllshire get over fifteen hundred pounds from the money set apart under the Insurance Act for Sanatoria, and might it not materially lighten the burden of the upkeep to Lorn District (Council) on account of the permanent erection of these shelters?

*Patrick's three remaining sons Cammie, Hugh and Jackie, 1915.*

Despite his scientific knowledge and his skills as a physician, Patrick, while providing wholesome fare and all the fresh air poor Hunter could endure, was defenceless against the disease. In the spring of 1914 correspondence from their friend Sam MacDougall indicates that Patrick and Mary were preparing to sell up and move to a better climate in hopes of improving Hunter's chances. These plans came to nought however. On 13 June 1914 Hunter died at the tender age of sixteen years.

For any parent, facing the death of a beloved child must be a fearful and harrowing experience. How much worse, then, for a doctor, one who has spent his life pursuing the health of others, who must stand by helpless while his first-born son, the boy in whom he has placed so many of his dreams for the future, dies slowly and painfully. Not until the eve of his departure to join his unit in the RAMC a year later could Patrick bring himself to enter the event in the family Bible.

# 9  *Healthy Minds in Healthy Bodies*

I N ACCORDANCE WITH his duties as a member of the School Board of Kilbrandon and Kilchattan Parish Council, Patrick regularly visited the schools in the district to examine the premises, reporting upon maintenance requirements, particularly those relating to health matters. In the course of these visits the teachers would bring to his attention certain children who because of their poor general health or specific problems of sight or hearing were not progressing as they should. They also reported upon children who came to school poorly clothed or obviously underfed. Patrick reported these incidents to the school board but to little effect. On a more personal level he might visit the homes and where possible do something to alleviate a problem by recourse to the provisions of the Poor Law. Where a child came to school with an infectious condition such as impetigo, an unsightly eruption of the skin caused by bacterial activity which unattended might lead to septicaemia, he arranged for the child's isolation and treatment within the classroom, realising that to exclude him from school altogether would merely compound one problem with another.

On his return from South Africa Patrick began in earnest to formalise his idea of a public school medical service supported financially by the Local Authority, which would ensure that every school child received regular examinations throughout his school life. These regular examinations would ascertain general health, identify deficiencies in eyesight and hearing and record any other chronic abnormalities whether genetic or accidental. Such conditions as were discovered by this general examination could then be treated, corrected and alleviated where necessary to ensure that each child had the best possible chance of benefiting fully from his or her education. By 1911, when Hunter was old enough to be enrolled in Watson's Academy and had already begun the long road which should have led him to a career in medicine, Patrick was ready to present to the county council the results of his research into the health of the school children in his care.

In the decade since his return from South Africa the doctor had kept meticulous records of examinations of the children of the Kilbrandon and Kilchattan parish, carried out in his own time and at his own expense. He was now in a position to produce a detailed paper outlining his proposals, in which he not only explained what should be done but how, by whom and at what cost. This latter was of particular significance. Patrick already had sufficient experience of the workings of the minds of the elected members of the Argyll County Council and their salaried officers, to know that this was the first and possibly the only aspect of his proposals which would be considered.

In his report he went to great lengths to show how action to correct deficiencies in the health of the school-age population would in the long run save the authority money by preventing more expensive remedial assistance in the future. It has to be remembered that although there were certain obligations placed upon county councils to supervise arrangements for disposal of sewage and household waste, to provide adequate supplies of safe, potable drinking water and to provide a means of controlling infectious and contagious disease, there was no health service as we know it today. Patients paid for the doctor's services themselves unless, through some insurance scheme such as that provided by the quarry companies and friendly societies, the fees were paid for them. Otherwise they had to rely upon public funds to help them by means of the parish-controlled Poor Laws. Patrick knew therefore that his proposals would be received with some scepticism. Nevertheless he went ahead, basing his proposition on surmise that prevention rather than cure was a sure way of saving money.

The following are the salient points taken from a long detailed document which Patrick presented to his immediate superior, Dr MacNeill, in 1911.

**A Scheme for the Regular Medical Inspection of School Children**
1. The scheme should be elastic and subject to change as experience dictates.
2. Preparatory visits would need to be made to schools to explain the nature of the

inspection, its purpose and the material requirements of the inspector in terms of accommodation and teacher support.

3. Time would have to be allocated for drafting and procuring the necessary documentation forms.

4. In the first year of the scheme all new entrants to the education system (five to six year-olds) would be examined and an attempt made to include in addition, all children of seven to eight years. There should be a thorough examination of every 'special' case brought forward by the teachers themselves (that is, cases of under nourishment, sickness, infestation, poor clothing, extreme poverty.)
[With so many islands included within the County of Argyll, travelling would inevitably present problems of time-tabling and costing. Patrick suggested that in the first year he should spend time researching all the travel possibilities, negotiating special rates for carriage and ferrying where necessary so that an efficient schedule of visits might be drawn up to provide the minimum expenditure of time and money.]

5. The Medical Officer appointed would require the services of a nurse/clerical assistant who would be responsible for preparing the school in advance for the doctor's visit, setting up the inspection room, drawing up the lists of children to be examined, conducting the routine sight and hearing tests and completing the reports on those requiring a follow-up.

6. The school nurse should be appointed as a servant of the local Authority with a well defined set of duties to be drawn up in the light of experience after the first few months. [He suggests a salary of £1 10s per week which is commensurate with the pay of trained nurses in non-infectious cases.] In addition there should be maintenance allowances and travelling expenses paid when away from home.

7. Initially all clerical work should be done by the medical officer and the nurse.

These proposals were submitted to the medical sub-committee of Argyll County Council on 11 Nov 1911.

Not only did Patrick have to convince the county councillors that his was a good idea but he also had to carry with him the school boards and the teachers themselves. Since the Education Scotland Act of 1873, schools had been subject to regular inspections by government officials whose job it was to ensure that standards of education were maintained at the highest levels. The annual visit from the government inspector (HMI) was anticipated with fear and trepidation by all concerned whether it be the members of the school board, who must account in detail for their expenditure of the government grant, the head teacher, the assistant masters and mistresses, or the pupils themselves. As this extract from the Oban High School logbook for 7 July 1882 indicates, the school was in a turmoil before the anticipated visit from the HMI :

Busy at work drilling up for the inspection. Attendance miserable in the senior department. A number of boys have left for work on condition that they would put in an appearance on the day of the inspection. Three of the pupil teachers absent all the week at the Normal Examination.

The inspector's report of 9–10 Jul 1883 gives an indication of the matters of greatest concern to the Department of Education, and upon which the annual grant was given.

The work of the school was interrupted a few months ago by an epidemic of measles. Which continued for some time to affect attendance and has reduced the number qualified for the examination. The progress made since the last inspection is however satisfactory on the whole all the departments giving evidence of earnest work on the part of the teachers. The general state of the infants department is very creditable and promising. In the Department comprising the second and third standards the order and discipline are much better than last year and the work is more efficiently done. Intelligence should however be better developed in the second standard. In the senior department the weakest points are the arithmetic for the fourth standard and the Composition of the fifth. The other work is on the whole well done but the Grammar of the fifth however not being quite so good as that of the other two standards. The answering in Geography and History is full and intelligent. Of the specific subjects professed, Physical Geography shows the least satisfactory results the others being very fair. The singing in the various departments is most pleasing. Needlework receives careful attention.

Aware of the disturbance to school routine of inspections by HMIs, Patrick did not imagine teachers would take kindly to yet another set of regular visits by a county medical officer. Head teachers might well consider such visits an intrusion into their well-ordered domains. He makes note of this difficulty in his preamble to the scheme and suggests a carefully programmed approach in order to reassure the teachers that there would be as little disturbance as possible to the regular routine of the school. To his surprise the doctor was to discover that the teachers actually welcomed the medical inspections because at last they had an opportunity to voice their own concerns about the condition of some of their pupils.

In some cases, however, the school boards were not so amenable to Patrick's proposals. Money was partly to blame for their lack of enthusiasm, the authority having decided that should the scheme be adopted, school boards would be charged at a cost of a few pence per school-age child in the parish. When presented with Patrick's proposal for their deliberation, the school board of Kilmartin Parish made it quite clear that they would prefer to continue with the occasional visit of their own local medical man who was, incidentally, himself a member of the board.

The following extract is taken from minutes of Kilmartin School Board:

15th Dec. 1911

The Clerk was instructed to communicate the following suggestion to the Scotch Education Dept.:

The School Board of Kilmartin have had under careful consideration the question of Medical Examination and Supervision of pupils attending Kilmartin School. They think that supervision by the local medical officer in this parish would at any rate be closer than any Medical Inspector for the County could possibly provide and they would be glad to be informed whether in the event of the local Doctor being appointed, he could be empowered to close the school forthwith in the event of the outbreak of some infectious disease in place of the present unsatisfactory arrangement whereby reference has to be made to a distant and possibly absent authority for permission to act.

This very narrow viewpoint shows how the Kilmartin Board had missed the point of Patrick's plan entirely. His intention was to ensure the good health of children from five to thirteen throughout the county using the system of inspections as an organ whereby general research into the condition of the children might be carried out and universal improvements inaugurated. To facilitate progress, the medical officer appointed would be empowered to take action where necessary. The closure of a school in the case of an epidemic was already dealt with by reference to the County Medical Officer of Health, Dr MacNeill.

On 9 Oct 1912 a minute of the School Board of the Island of Ghiga records the receipt of a copy of a letter from the clerk of the board to the Argyll Secondary Education Committee dated 6 Sep 1912, relating to a scheme for Medical Inspection and Supervision of School Children. The letter was read and considered:

The Board, while strongly objecting to the scheme which they believe will prove to be insufficient with regards to the health of the children and much more expensive as regards the salary, travelling expenses and possible pension of the gentleman appointed, accept the scheme with reluctance because they understand that were they to hold out for a more sensible way for which they have striven, their constituents would be punished by having to contribute to the Committee's scheme as well as to pay for their own. This is a specimen of local Government of which the board do not approve.

For Kilchrenan and Dalavich School Board the scheme for the examination and supervision of school children was presented on 29 Apr 1911 and met with the approval of the board. Here, as in many of the more remote parishes, there was no doctor nearby and sometimes even where there was a practitioner, he was not necessarily as conscientious as Patrick Gillies. Many doctors took a rural practice only as a last resort and were disconsolate at not obtaining something more lucrative or prestigious; some drank, others were simply not up to the job. Whatever the reason, it is interesting to note that this school board at least welcomed Patrick's plan.

One of the key points of the plan, which he used in trying to persuade his medical colleagues to support him, was that the views of the medical officer for schools would have more weight with the county councillors than would those of a local general practitioner. It was also possible, according to Gillies, for the Schools' MO to override the decisions of a school board if necessary. An example of the kind of problem Patrick felt might be overcome is given by the following extracts from the minutes of Saddle and Skipness School Board, dated 26 Jun 1911.* It appears that the school board had refused the local doctor's order to exclude children suffering from infectious disease. This was despite Dr Christie of Carradale having issued appropriate medical certificates. Since it was against the law for parents to keep their children away from school without the consent of the board, the infected pupils had remained in class, a danger to the rest of their classmates. On 3 June Dr Christie had written a letter to the Scotch Education Department complaining that the school board was interfering in matters which were his prerogative. It was, he contended, his responsibility to report all cases of infectious disease to the chief medical officer for the county, and in the name of that officer, to issue exclusion notices when necessary.

**Saddle and Skipness School Board minute of 26th June:**
The clerk produced a letter dated 21st June 1911 from the Education Dept. with reference to the recent epidemic of chickenpox in the district of Carradale and Torrisdale. The Board after consideration authorised the Chairman and clerk to reply that the order given to the headteacher of Carradale school on 30th May last that he was not to exclude from school children coming from infected homes but not themselves affected, was never meant to be a permanent order and as the school was closed on the 21st June for the summer holidays it has now been withdrawn.

The Board then studied the requirements of the Education Scotland Act of 1908 Section 17(6) and the Department's circular dated 31st March 1909 and having had a conference with Dr Christie invited him to perform the necessary inspections under the Act. The Scotch Education Dept was duly informed.

---

* For these extracts from minutes of the various school boards I am indebted to Mr Murdo McDonald, until recently the county archivist for Argyll and Bute. His help in tracking down references to Patrick's scheme for the medical inspection of school children has been invaluable.

What seems clear from this incident is that this board's members had never consulted the terms of the Act of Parliament passed in 1908 which required school boards to observe the rules of exclusion of infective school pupils. Their treatment of the doctor in this case was unpardonable and Patrick's contention was that the matter might have been dealt with speedily and without involving the Scotch Education Department if there had been an MO for Schools available for consultation!

When the same board was asked to consider Patrick's proposals, the arrogance and ignorance with which they approached them was surpassed only by their extremely parochial attitude to the whole idea. Having quite clearly failed to understand the purpose of the scheme and the intentions behind the appointment of a County MO for Schools, they met to discuss the proposal with extraordinary results. On 2 Mar 1912 documents in connection with a scheme for the Medical Inspection of School Children were placed before them, sent for consideration by Argyll Secondary Education Committee. Among the papers was a statement indicating that it was proposed to have one medical inspector for the whole county who would be remunerated at the rate of four hundred pounds per year, with travelling expenses. The cost to the school boards would probably be at the rate of one shilling per annum per scholar. As the minutes of the meeting indicate:

> The Board, after consideration, declined to adopt this scheme as in their opinion it would be an utter impossibility for the County Medical Officer to satisfactorily discharge his duties in respect of their parish (Saddle and Skipness) owing to the length of the parish being twenty five miles and the scattered nature of the population. The meeting was of the opinion that the medical inspection of school children could be better managed by themselves engaging a local practitioner. The Board on the motion of the Chairman unanimously appointed Dr Christie as medical inspector of schools under their charge and at a salary of twenty pounds per annum.

Bearing in mind their recent debacle over the treatment of infectious disease, the minute also included reference to the provision of certificates to those children excluded from school by reason of infectious disease. This committee, who quite clearly considered themselves experts in all things, then proceeded to lay down the duties of a medical inspector for schools. The clerk was instructed to send a copy of the resolution to Dr Christie and to inform the secretary of the Scotch Board of Education of their decision. Had someone only read the papers correctly, they would have realised that the proposal emanated from the county's secretary for secondary education and was nothing to do with the Scotch Office in Westminster!

In due course a letter was received from a somewhat mystified clerk to the Scotch Education Department on the question of the board's appointment of Dr Christie to a position it knew nothing about. This letter indicated that, since the department had no alternative scheme at present for the medical inspection of school children, they had no objection to what the board proposed. It was however the county council which had produced the scheme and they most certainly did object to the action of the Saddle and Skipness Board!

Protesting volubly to the Scotch Education Department that that body had no business interfering in decisions made by Argyll County Council with regard to the appointment of staff, the chairman of the Committee for Secondary Education with the backing of the chairman of the County Council, demanded that the clerk to the Scotch Office of Education withdraw its letter agreeing to the appointment of Dr Christie. Within days the clerk to the Saddle and Skipness School Board received a letter from the Scotch Education Department withdrawing its earlier letter of compliance. As a result, the board immediately terminated the appointment of Dr Christie as Schools' MO for the parish.

Throughout Argyll school boards were now discussing Patrick's scheme with reactions which differed according to the degree of attention each gave to the detail of the Gillies paper. Also, reactions were governed by the priorities of individual members of the boards. Nevertheless, whether they were for or against Patrick's plan, the boards were now clamouring for action of one kind or another.

On 2 May 1912, the Public Health Committee of Argyll County Council had before it a scheme for the medical inspection of school children, which had been submitted by the secretary of the secondary education committee of Argyll County Council. This body had adopted Patrick's proposal without any significant omissions or alterations.

The Committee was instructed to take the advice of the county medical officer of health in making the appointment and because Dr McNeill, who had been receiving Patrick's very detailed annual reports since his first in 1894, thoroughly approved of his younger colleague, there was no competition for the post. Dr Patrick Gillies was duly appointed.

# 10 The Medical Officer for Schools

HIS LETTER OF acceptance to the county council indicates that Patrick had been given a starting date of 1 Nov 1912. This did not suit him at all for he realised that if he did not perform the first inspection, that of the new intake of children – five to six year olds – at the very beginning of the new school year, which was in the middle of August, he was unlikely to be in a position to present a complete set of results in his first year in office. Consequently his very first letter in his new post was controversial!

Dunmore House, Easdale

The Secretary, Argyll Health Board

Dear Mr Sinclair,

I duly received your letter of yesterday and beg to thank the committee for the honour conferred upon me. I hope my work may be to their satisfaction.

It would not be well I think in the current year at any rate to depart from the recognised system of School Inspection and I could send you copies of the schedules, cards, instructions etc. which we generally used.

Perhaps the sub-committee wish my opinion on more than this and if so would you indicate under what heads my proposals are required.

As the year, for purposes of school inspection, ends on the 31st July it would be important to begin the work at as early a date as possible after that time. In this way we may have a distinct age division of the children examined all over the County in the first year and avoid overlapping of work for next year. If I do not enter upon duties until 11th November I would like to mention now that little of the actual work of inspection could be undertaken before the New Year. There would possibly be at least a month's preliminary work organising, printing instructions and exchanging preliminary correspondence with schools.

It is immaterial to me when I begin work as in any case, I shall be required to provide a substitute here until arrangements for this parish are completed. I could undertake the preliminary work at any time, should the sub-committee so wish.

I am yours faithfully,

Patrick H Gillies

Although he was able to take on some of the new work at the earlier date he had suggested, Patrick found in effect that tying up all his other activities in the parish was to take much longer than he had anticipated. Patrick's appointment to Local Authority office necessitated his resignation from several of his other commitments, with the quarrying communities on Seil and Luing, with the parish council and the committee administering the Poor Law and with the school board. In the circumstances, it is hardly surprising that it was not until 17 Jan 1913 that Patrick wrote his last letter as the MO for the parish of Kilbrandon and Kilchattan. Typically it was one expressing concern about the spread of infectious disease amongst the school children of the district.

Some children living in Balvicar village had been attending school at the Ardencaple School, Clachan. At the same time, certain Clachan children were attending Easdale Public School.

The Clerk
Kilbrandon and Kilchattan School Board.                              Easdale 17.1.13

Dear Sir,

With regard to the underwritten children you are requested in accordance with previous minutes of your Board and instructions from the Local Authority on Public Health, to see that children from the Balvicar Village and all those living south of a line generally below the Clachan Stream, attend Easdale Village School.
I would not have interfered in this matter were the children in question leaving school soon but the habit must not be continued as on previous occasions, the Public Health Authority has been able by the strict observance of this rule to confine such epidemics as whooping cough and measles to one district.
With regard to children from Clachan attending Easdale School
MacDonald     Age 13     9/12     Balvicar
Shaw Fiona          13     10/12     Balvicar
As these are generally senior scholars, the same danger is not incurred and the restriction would not apply during an epidemic.
I may point out that the MacDougall children of John MacDougall are already cases in point.
Let me hear that this matter is attended to without delay.

Yours faithfully

Patrick H Gillies

There was in addition some delay in appointing Patrick's successor to the Easdale practice. Lord Breadalbane, although clearly pleased that Patrick had at last achieved his goal of a public appointment, was anxious to get the best possible replacement doctor for the parish. On 12 Dec 1912 he wrote to Mr Buckley, his factor at Taymouth Castle, concerning the appointment of a medical officer for the Easdale quarries:

> I am certainly truly thankful that you have been asked to select a doctor and that it is not this time being left to the quarry people to do so. On a former occasion a gentleman came to the district that I would certainly have hesitated except under most exceptional circumstances or in the event of a bad accident to call in.
>
> Whether a man not knowing the district and never having had any experience of Scotland will settle down in a place like Toberonochy is a matter which is worthy of consideration. I quite admit that the means in the past of getting a doctor in case of emergency could be improved and that Easdale was not the best place for a medical man to reside, the house at Cuan Ferry [Ballachuan House] being certainly preferable and further having the advantage of being near the hospital. Speaking quite candidly I do not think that Toberonochy would be a very suitable place for a medical man for the whole district to reside. Moreover there would always be the difficulty of his getting his horse and trap across on the ferry while if he kept a motor that is to say unless it was a motor bicycle, he would not be able to get it over at all.
>
> I cannot help thinking that if a telephone could be got into the doctor's house at Cuan Ferry, seeing there are telegraph offices at Cullipool, Toberonochy, Easdale, Balvicar, Melfort and Kilninver and further looking to the wants of the whole district, that Cuan is the best place for the medical man to reside.

In a letter dated 12 Dec 1912 Breadalbane, replying to a request from Patrick to extend the sub-tenancy of Ballachuan House so that the present occupants might remain there until their new property is ready, writes to Patrick denying him an extension. He advises him that Mr MacLean Buckley of Luing is anxious to appoint a doctor to reside at Toberonochy and serve the quarry communities on Luing. Breadalbane is now more than ever concerned that a doctor be appointed for the entire district and that he be installed in Ballachuan House as soon as possible. He is even prepared to pay for the installation of a telephone if that will help matters along.

Patrick's old sparring partners the quarry masters on Luing had seized upon his resignation as an opportunity to appoint a doctor of their own choosing. After several abortive attempts to replace Dr Gillies, they had elected to employ a French doctor, M. Collenette, from one of the French-African colonies. The gentleman was dark skinned, and bearing in mind that coloured people were a rare occurrence anywhere but in the ports and larger cities of the British Isles at the beginning of the twentieth century, the proposal to introduce an African doctor to the inhabitants of the island of Luing seemed to Breadalbane to be both outrageous and impracticable. On 4 Jan Breadalbane writes in reply to Patrick's report of the appointment of M. Colenette to the post of MO for Luing:

> Only fancy a Baboo Doctor in Luing, with his white trousers, the proverbial frock coat, not too new, which these gentlemen invariably wear, topped by a turban and in his hand a cane with a magnificent mount on the top of it, usually made of tin. I wonder if the gentleman in question will be accompanied by a black nurse: whether he will come equipped with a lascar crew to row him out to the islands when his medical services are demanded. No doubt opportunity will be given to those in the district to learn an Oriental language and it is not beyond the bounds of possibility that you may even yet see old McInnes and me pouring over some Oriental Grammar for the purpose of making ourselves understood. While you, in your new official capacity may be called upon to inspect some black babies in the local schools. What a joyful picture for us all to look forward to! [. . .] I really should like to be a fly on the ceiling to see the first visit the new medical officer for Luing pays to some old Highland lady [. . .] I presume that the currency at Easdale will in future be reckoned by rupees instead of bawbees.

Such words could not be uttered in public today; although written in a joking vein, they indicate only too clearly the extent of the ignorance and prejudice of the day, even amongst the better educated and wealthier members of society. Breadalbane mixes up lascars, coolies and black Africans as though they are all the same and his prejudice does not end with workers from overseas. In a letter to Patrick dated 12 Dec 1912, he says, 'At the same time I cannot help thinking that to import someone from London to a place like Toberonochy is very foolish. An Englishman will never settle down in a place like Toberonochy or even Easdale.' How wrong he was. Today nearly fifty percent of the population of the Slate Islands is of English descent!

In his letter to Gillies dated 8 Jan 1913, Breadalbane congratulates the doctor on his choice of Dr Henderson Cassels for the Easdale practice but goes on to comment on the appointment of M. Collenette to the Luing practice:

> Poor old gentleman. It's rather rough on him sending him to Luing. As you so justly point out under existing circumstances the Lascar would be of no service. I hope our worthy friend Mr McDonald at the School House will now get in a supply of French Grammars and Dictionaries for the old women of Luing so that they may make their complaints known to M. Collenette. I am afraid from your description you will not have an opportunity of examining any little darkies at the schools.
> Chaffing apart, it really is rather sad the whole affair, to say nothing of it being extremely foolish. Luing has certainly not been fortunate in the past in the selection of its medical practitioner and as far as one can judge the new appointment must be as

unsuccessful as most of those preceding it. I expect what will happen is that after M. Collenette sees the place, the house and the people he will pack his bags and return South! If he comes soon (January or February) I should say there is little doubt of it.

Believe me

Yours truly,  BREADALBANE

For whatever reason, M. Collenette never took up his post and the appointed medical practioner was duly installed at Ballachuan House, which remained the doctor's residence until the mid twentieth century. In the 1950s the Easdale Practice was housed at Balvicar House until the present doctor's residence, Fin-laggan, was built at Oban Seil by Dr Willie McKerrel.

Patrick was now free to take up his new post, with his office in Oban, at that time the administrative centre of Argyll. The lady appointed to be Patrick's school nurse was a Miss Elizabeth Simpson. She was to become as well known in the county as the medical officer himself. During the early years of the scheme it was her gentle diplomacy and careful arrangements which ensured that visits passed without rancour even though, particularly in very small schools with perhaps only the one teacher, the medical inspection caused considerable disruption of classes.

Once the teachers began to see the benefit of the inspections they welcomed the visits of the doctor who could relieve them of the burdens of neglected or brutalised children and those in dire poverty. Here at last was a tangible being to whom one might turn with what often appeared to be insoluble problems, and because Patrick was anxious to see the scheme successfully off the ground he never spared himself in the performance of his duties. His was the ear which heard the teachers' concerns and he was the one person who might provide answers to these when all else failed.

Patrick quickly began to realise, however, that it was one thing to identify a problem but another altogether to have something done to resolve it. Children with defective eyesight for example required spectacles, but who was to pay if the family could not afford it? Worse than this was the problem of checking to see that the inspector's orders had actually been carried out. A whole year between one visit and the next was a long time in the school life of a child and delay in rectifying some condition which inhibited learning could mean a large slice of the pupil's education was omitted before matters were put to rights. In due course, local clinics were set up where children could be referred for treatment immediately after the visit of the school doctor but it took a few years before Local Authorities could be persuaded of the efficacy of this expensive innovation! Patrick submitted his first annual report as schools medical officer for the county on 30 Sep 1913. Outlining the extent of his work, he described his region of operation, which was the entire county of Argyll at that time, as being 1,990,471 acres, extending from Ardnamurchan to Kintyre (115 miles) and Tiree to the Perthshire border (90 miles). The county's population of 69,063 included those living on 41 inhabited islands as well as those on the mainland. The school population for the years 1911 and 1912 was approximately ten thousand. Many of the more remote schools had pupil numbers of less than ten.

Having taken up his duties on 11 Nov 1911, during the first year Patrick had examined only those infants attending school for the first time and those who would be leaving at the end of the school year. This procedure had caused a considerable amount of concern amongst the parents who felt that they were entitled to an examination for all their children. Patrick had to spend time in every location explaining his reasons. For the older children this was the last opportunity for him to record the condition of their health before they disappeared from the registers. Hopefully some at least of the defects might be corrected before they left school. On the other hand, it was logical to begin with the youngest intake whose progress could then be measured year upon year. In Patrick's scheme, as the years went by every child would receive at least two examinations before leaving school. Those who had been found to require treatment in their first year would be followed up in school visits of subsequent years.

During this first year three hundred and thirty-nine boys and three hundred and forty-one girls were identified by the teachers as having particular needs. Of these, six hundred children were found to have defects requiring treatment and follow-up. Of a total of three thousand children seen under the regular inspection, seven hundred and fifty-eight boys and nine hundred and thirty-five girls were recommended for further examination or treatment. Tests were carried out for sight, weight, hearing, nose and throat, and heart and lungs. Heads were inspected for the presence of vermin. For sight tests a distance of twenty feet was required. Few country schools had a room of this size and the test was often carried out in a corridor or even in the open air! The remainder of the examination could be carried out in a much smaller room, often the head teacher's own study. The general state of cleanliness of each child's body and the condition and suitability of clothing was noted. Parents were invited to be present at the examination although Patrick found this a nuisance since it was usually the parents of the healthy, better fed and clothed children who took up this option, and in the presence of their parents the children were invariably less well behaved!

Patrick was well aware of the importance of keeping the teachers on his side and endeavoured to cause them the least possible disruption during his visits. Once the scheme had been under way for a year, Patrick found his visits anticipated with a surprising amount of pleasure. Teachers were quick to point out those parents who made a very particular effort when the doctor was coming and whose children appeared in an almost unrecognisably clean condition for the occasion. Patrick's response to such reports was that 'at least the children got a wash once a year!' He was however concerned to find children who, although free from vermin on the day of the examination, showed every sign of recent infestation and he tried to explain to erring parents that it was useless putting clean clothes on a dirty child. He advocated a sure recipe for the removal of nits. Paraffin oil, the cruder the better, should be applied to the head with all due caution on three successive nights. This destroyed the ova and loosened the nits so that they could then be removed by ordinary washing in soap and water. Although a drastic and very smelly method, this he considered preferable to the creams and lotions available at the time which, while destroying the adult parasite, had little or no effect upon the eggs themselves.

Many of the children displayed the skin diseases associated with poverty and dirt – impetigo, ringworm, and scabies – while other complaints, believed even then to be hereditary – eczema, psoriasis and pytiriasis – were often exacerbated by neglect and ignorance of the most suitable treatment. Lupus, associated with infection by the tuberculin bacillus, was associated with overcrowded living conditions and cross infection between family members. These cases required immediate treatment and in certain instances isolation. It was Patrick's duty to report these issues to parents, the Local Authority and the local GP, but he had no means in the early days of following up such cases to ensure that his instructions were carried out.

As early as 1912 Patrick noted that there was a distinct difference in the dentition of country children brought up on plentiful supplies of milk and those in the towns, who displayed alarming degrees of dental caries through too much sugar consumption.

Although tonsils usually shrink in early adolescence they may remain as harbourers of bacteria and cause debilitating illness. Today, with antibiotics readily available, extraction is a rare occurrence, but at the beginning of the twentieth century the only treatment for enlarged tonsils was extraction. Patrick's report contains many references to the need for such treatment, but, again, he was unable to ensure that his orders were carried out. He found a high percentage of enlarged cervical glands in the infants (37.3 per cent), but as this might indicate a defensive battle taking place against bacterial invaders, which would provide immunity later in life, he did not suggest extraction at such an early age. On examining school leavers in early adolescence, he found this figure to have dropped to 16.42 per cent, justifying his suspicions that swollen tonsils in five year olds did not necessarily lead to chronic infection later on.

This was only his first year of carrying out such examinations so he was careful not to make presumptuous conclusions from his findings, but it did seem to Patrick that this was a clear indication that both tonsils and cervical glands were a defensive mechanism in young children that should be left intact on the assumption that they would reduce or disappear completely during adolescence. During the following years he was to confirm that this shrinkage of both cervical glands and tonsils on the approach of adolescence was the norm, a clinical fact that appears not to have been noted previously in the medical world. It was the meticulous collection of data such as this, from which more general conclusions could be reached about the health of Scotland's children, that was to justify the continuance of the schools' medical services after the hiatus brought about by the onset of war in 1914.

Patrick began his examinations in the parishes of Kilbrandon and Kilninver where the procedures differed little from those employed by him previously. Here there were efficient weighing machines which he had installed himself. He was to find that while the newer, secondary schools were quite well equipped with weighing apparatus, primary schools had been issued with an inferior device and side schools, nothing at all. Almost at once he had to put in a request for a set of scales which he could carry around with him. He placed great emphasis upon the results of bodily measurements, relating height and weight to nutrition, housing and general social condition. He was also able after a few years to present to the Local Authority a definitive statement upon the relationship between performance in the classroom and the general health of the child. He pointed out that, although it was generally the poorer children who suffered from malnutrition and that the majority of these lived in rural areas, in the towns children were defective as a result of unsuitable nutrition rather than poverty. In 1912 50 per cent more children in town schools were found to be defective nutritionally than in the country schools! Patrick suggested that this was due to the better quality of the fresh, home-produced food of country children, even though their daily intake might be less than that of town children.

Patrick also commented upon the numbers of school children who worked before and after school hours. He had found that some began work as early as six-thirty, arriving in time for school but without having had breakfast. They were then inattentive through tiredness. In advocating the passing of a by-law restricting the working hours of school-age children Patrick was to offend not only those parents who depended upon the small earnings of their children but also the local employers who relied upon this cheap source of labour! It has to be remembered that the employment of children under the age of eleven had only been outlawed a few decades earlier. Now another whittling away of the labour force was being proposed!

Patrick's nurse, Elizabeth Simpson, remained with him throughout his tenure of the post of county schools' MO. When, in 1915, Patrick joined the RAMC and went to war, Miss Simpson carried on with the routine testing of hearing and eyesight and the inspection for infestation by such unwanted visitors as head lice and bedbugs. Eventually, however, when the war seemed to be prolonged indefinitely, the schools medical service was suspended until hostilities ceased. Nurse Simpson joined the Queen Alexandra's Nursing Service for the duration of hostilities but by the time Patrick returned to his county post in 1920 he was delighted to find that it was again Miss Simpson who was to be his right-hand woman.

By 1915 the public had had time to form its own ideas about the success or otherwise of the schools medical service. Naturally enough it was those who paid the rates who paid greatest attention to the manner in which their money was being spent, as this letter to *The Scotsman* of 4 Jan 1915 indicates:

> I as many another, hoped that the medical inspection would be beneficial inasmuch as it might determine the working capacity of the child and prevent the child with some physical weakness from suffering through the strain of competition with the

healthy. So far as I can ascertain this is not put into effect and it seems doubtful if any attempt has been made in this direction. It is apparent that more statistics are required. Has the average school attendance increased or decreased? Have zymotic diseases increased or decreased? Are such diseases as ringworm, impetigo, scabies, pediculosis of less frequent occurrence? Has the average intelligence improved? These are questions which every ratepayer has a right to have answered. The enormous expenditure on medical inspection and treatment deserves some tangible return and it should now be possible to show the benefits derived. If such benefits exist then they should be weighed in the balance with the expenditure and the ratepayer should seriously consider if the result justifies the means [. . .] Frederick Porter

This seems pretty harsh criticism of a scheme which had been fully operational for only two years. Even if every school's medical officer in the country was as meticulous in the gathering of statistics as was Patrick Gillies, it was still far too soon to be making comparative studies. What the scheme had revealed, however, was the poor living conditions, inadequate clothing and inadequate nutrition of a large majority of Scotland's school children. The economic position of the country's workforce was the responsibility of government and employers, not of the medical officer for schools!

Given a further ten years during most of which records were kept, Patrick was able to show a steady improvement in certain aspects of the children's condition. In 1913 he reported of 1,706 boys examined 1.76 per cent had head lice and in 3.11 per cent their bodies were verminous, while the girls showed equivalent figures of 21.05 per cent with head lice but only 1.98% with body lice (bites from bedbugs and viral or bacteriologically induced lesions such as impetigo). In the 1921 report these figures had become 0.38 per cent of boys presenting with head lice and 1.68 per cent verminous bodies, while the girls' figures had fallen to 13.13 per cent with head lice and 1.35 per cent with body vermin. The problem of head lice has always been more apparent in girls than in boys, largely because of their longer and more elaborate hairstyles. Other figures showed an increase in undernourished and underdeveloped children, and these, together with increases in the incidence of TB and other diseases of poverty and overcrowding, were an indication of the onset of the depression which was to prevail for a further decade. Where the school inspections proved most useful in those early days was in flagging up the trends in social development or decline.

During his absence on War Department duties, his work as schools' MO was never far from Patrick's thoughts. Perhaps this was his way of detaching himself from the gruesome carnage of battle. Whatever his reasons, in 1916 he sent a paper to the chairman of the Board of Education outlining his thoughts on the future operation of the Schools Medical Service. When Patrick had first formulated his ideas for the regular inspection of schoolchildren it had been with the clear intention that, not only would defects in the children's health be identified, they should be treated and where necessary followed up until the child left school. What he found during the early years was that despite reports and recommendations to parents and local GPs some children never received treatment. It was often the poorest and most vulnerable pupils who fell through the net, continuing to be neglected. Having commented on the failure of the schools' medical inspection programme to ensure that defects in the children's health were being attended to satisfactorily, Patrick pointed out that the problem was largely one of communication between the various authorities. This was due in part to the fact that administration of the programme came under the umbrella of the Education Department while the provision of treatments, isolation of infective cases and matters of poor sanitation, came under the Public Health Committee. There were two budgets over which both parties could fight and it was only too easy to lay any delay or neglect in attending to the children's problems at the door of the other party!

In a sense, Patrick's concerns about the lack of follow-up after school medical inspections had already been anticipated. In 1915 a number of school clinics were introduced in England providing general treatments including dentistry and eye tests. In his 1916 report, Patrick costed the setting up and running of similar clinics in Oban, Campbeltown, Dunoon and Kilmun. He estimated the cost to the county as £1,235 [approximately £180,000 today] and proposed that the money to provide the service might be deducted from the grant presently given to local practitioners. On the assumption that the Department of Health would cover 60 per cent of the money, the cost to the Education Department would be £494 per annum [say, £75,000 today].

In his 1920–21 report, written a year after returning to duty with Argyll, Patrick pointed out the inconsistency of provision of health care throughout life. Prenatal care was the responsibility of the local Health Authority. From birth to age five patients were either taken care of through the father's National Insurance (panel) arrangements, dealt with privately or came under the Poor Law provision. From five to fourteen years, a child was in the care of the Education Authority through the Medical Inspection of Schools. From fourteen to sixteen there was no protection unless the adolescent sought work in an institution which provided medical cover for its staff. From sixteen to retirement the National Insurance Scheme (1911) provided health cover through an Insurance Committee. Post-retirement, it was back to the Poor Law.

Patrick's contention was that it was not until children were gathered together in school that they came under the direct care of the state and that by the age of five years any mental or physical defects had already become well established and were consequently harder to rectify. He considered the solution to the problem would be to transfer responsibility for the health of the nation's children from Education to the Department of Health, where it strictly belonged, a system which would offer a smooth passage through the various stages of life and provide continuity of all relevant records. The downside was that the schools might be less willing to co-operate with officials from outside the Education Department, but Patrick felt this would be small price to pay in order to remove the current muddle.

He drew up yet another plan advocating a centralised medical officer for schools, answerable to the Health Board and aided by a full-time nurse, the jobs of both to be largely administrative. The schools' MO would plan and implement schemes designed to improve the health of school children generally and prevent rather than cure disease. The nurse would correlate and advise on the work of those conducting the medical inspections in the schools. Local medical officers, appointed by the Health Board from amongst the existing GPs, would be responsible for the school medical inspections, for carrying out any necessary treatments of defects and for reporting local sanitary problems. For this they would receive a fixed sum according to the population of the practice.

In 1920, twenty-eight years before the inauguration of Aneurin Bevan's National Health Service, Dr Patrick Gillies laid down his proposals for a national health scheme:

> Unfortunately we lack any definition of what a state medical service is but if it means that all medical practitioners are to be whole time employees of the state, I am quite sure that the times are not ripe for it. I doubt whether they will ever be. If on the other hand those advocating a state service really mean that the state ought to co-operate with the profession in providing a more complete medical service for the community, then they may regard me as a sympathiser. Rightly or wrongly the state has entered upon a path of supplying expert assistance in respect of treatment as well as prevention notably in tuberculosis and venereal diseases. There are two ways along which events must inevitably advance. Either there will be provided a whole time staff of experts organised as a branch of the Civil or Municipal Services or the profession will agree to

undertake part time service in co-operation with the state. I need hardly say that my sympathy is in favour of the latter alternative.

In 1948 when the British Medical Association was negotiating with the government over the terms of employment of doctors in the National Health Service, it was precisely upon these matters that the debate rested. Patrick never lived to see his forecast implemented but his son, Alexander Campbell Gillies MD, was to practise under the National Health Service from its inception until his retirement in 1966. Cammie had very mixed feelings about the National Health Service and often expressed the opinion that his father might have had rather different thoughts about it had he lived to experience the system in operation.

*Outside Easdale School shortly before the Second World War. Patrick would have been delighted to see this picture of children showing every sign of good health and well being. With them are the minister and some of their parents.*

# 11 A Man of the People

IN THE YEARS since Patrick had taken up the Easdale practice, what spare time he had found from his medical practice, his farm and his family had been given over to the interests of the community as a whole. He was as anxious to see the men and their families well housed and fed as he was to keep them fit for the strenuous work they did. Uppermost in his mind was the removal of that ignorance which deprived so many working men of the rights and privileges which were their entitlement. While he wanted to see all men literate and numerate he also saw the importance of giving them access to the scientific and literary information which he himself enjoyed. For this reason he supported fully the work of the Easdale Literary and Scientific Association, which had been set up in 1860 by John Whyte, the manager of the Easdale Quarries, and Patrick's father, Dr Hugh Gillies. One of the first things Patrick did on his return to Easdale in 1893, having completed his medical studies, was to join with the manager of Easdale quarries, Angus Whyte, the minister and his good friend Sam MacDougall, the inspector of the poor, to revive the Easdale Scientific and Literary Association, which had lately become moribund. Under Patrick's chairmanship the association entered a decade of successful activity which was to end only at the outbreak of war in 1914.

At a meeting of the association held on 23 Jan 1904 Dr Patrick Gillies was chairing and the subject of the meeting was an application to the Coates Foundation for a supply of technical and literary books in the Gaelic language. These it seems were supplied in due course together with a bookcase suitable for

A Young Men's Temperance League outing, c.1900. This was one of the many organizations set up in the late nineteenth century to curb the excessive consumption of alcohol. While they may not have entirely wiped out the evils of drink, such associations provided a platform for a variety of entertainments and social occasions. Lectures, slide shows, musical evenings and soirees took place in the Volunteers' Drill Hall while picnics and outings to places of interest were arranged in the summer months. Both Patrick and his wife Mary were very much involved in arrangements for events held to raise money, for instance, for the Volunteers' summer camp. The annual Summer Ball was the highlight of the year, usually attended by His Lordship's Captain of Ardmaddy, the Factor, Mr Campbell. On this occasion Breadalbane always provided a haunch of venison as his contribution to the feast.

their storage. The only stipulation that came with the gift of books was that the association should receive two lectures from a person appointed by the Coates Foundation and that admission to these lectures should be free. Much to the alarm of the committee members, the foundation informed them they would be sending a Mr Forsyth, Professor of Elocution at Glasgow University, to give the lectures. Not knowing how their membership of tough quarrymen would receive this gentleman, they were quite relieved to receive in addition a request for musical entertainment arranged by the men themselves, to be included in

The quarry at Cullipool on the Island of Luing, c.1890. The steep angle of the slate beds meant that quarrying took place almost vertically; the pits produced by this method reaching depths of up to 70 metres. Since the men were working well below sea level there was a constant problem of seawater seeping through the rocks and this, together with the prodigious rainfall in the area, necessitated the constant pumping of water from

the workings. Once the quarries were abandoned they quickly filled forming the beautiful, tranquil pools seen most clearly in the aerial photograph in the introduction. Slate was removed from the depths of the quarry in this case by means of a vertical lift. Other quarries, particularly on Easdale Island, employed an inclined plane: two parallel tracks upon which counterbalancing trucks were hauled up and down by a steam-driven winch.

*When the 1st Argyll and Bute Artillery Volunteers were inaugurated in 1860 it quickly became clear that training would be hampered by the inclement weather. Two drill halls were erected on the islands, and this at Ellenabeich had a floor strengthened to withstand a full-sized cannon.*

the programme. The meeting, held on 16 Mar, was attended by more than one hundred quarrymen and, contrary to expectation, Professor Forsyth proved to be an accomplished and entertaining speaker who kept the company rocking in the aisles for most of the evening, his long string of hilarious anecdotes being interspersed by some pretty rowdy singing and playing arranged by Archie McLean and Archie MacKay, quarrymen from Luing.

In order to raise funds for the expansion of the library and to pay for further outside speakers the association held many soirees, ceilidhs and an annual ball, providing a varied social life in which not only the men but the women and children also could participate. It was at events such as this, as well as the regular meetings of the men, that Patrick was to get to know the community he served; in this relaxed atmosphere people spoke most freely of their day-to-day concerns. The association continued to flourish until the quarries at Easdale closed in 1911.

On his return from South Africa, Patrick had resumed his position as surgeon to the 1st Argyll (Easdale) Artillery Volunteers and in recognition of his Army service he was promoted to the rank of major. As company surgeon he was never over-taxed by his medical duties. The members of the Volunteers were a hale and hearty bunch and, apart from the odd crushed finger, the occasional cracked wrist and sprained ankle, not to mention more than a few powder burns, Patrick had little to occupy him surgically even when they went away

*1st Argyll & Bute Volunteers in a considerable state of undress at their summer camp held in Campbeltown c.1905.*

to camp for a week every summer. He seems to have also acted as treasurer and company clerk, for his letter book carries a detailed account of the logistics of taking a company of the Volunteers to one such camp. In 1903 the company commander and quarry manager was Major Wilson.

**Report on the 1st Argyll and Bute Artillery Volunteer Company's attendance at Barry Camp Summer, June 1903**

The team of Volunteers which represented No1 and No2 Company Argyll and Bute Artillery Volunteers at Barry Camp returned home on Thursday last after an eventful and successful sojourn there. It was not until Saturday however that the full measure of their success was known and it is a source of great satisfaction to their well wishers to know that the good name of these companies has been more than maintained and that they have secured some of the best prizes available.

The team which left here under the command of Sgts. H. McLean and D. MacPherson, was joined on their arrival at camp by their commanding officer, Major Wilson. After a day of rest the real work of the team began. In the drill and gun laying competitions they did well and although not successful in obtaining a prize they had the highest number of marks scored [in total] up to the day of their leaving camp. In repristory work [repositioning the gun] they again showed their capability, taking the 1st prize of £3.00 and making a total of 92 points out of a possible 100. In the long ships and boating the favourites were A team which until last year had had an unbroken record. Sgt. Dugald MacPherson who commanded the winning team last year was again No1. and once again found his capability as a careful and accurate non-commissioned officer: cool-headed and cautious in every detail of this important aspect of artillery work. In parbuckling [dismantling an artillery gun, moving its pieces over a series of obstacles, and then reassembling and firing it] the Easdale men also cleared 1st prize making all the 100 marks possible. Sgt. McLean and Corp. Matthew Livingston were in command, the former mounting and the latter dismantling the gun. Admirable work was done by both NCOs with the exactness and promptitude that won the admiration of all onlookers.

Patrick then gave a detailed account of the expenses incurred by those representing the company, a team of twenty men. No doubt the officers paid their own expenses.

| **Money received** | **Money expended** |
|---|---|
| Cheque £10.00 | Fares W. Buddon from Oban  £9.9.2 |
| Cheque £5.00 | Captain Dewar for ship 'Dunlop' £3.0.0 |
| Men's subs £7.10.0 [They | Cash to Sgt MacLean £3.0.0 |
| paid 7/6 each ie 38p] | Remittance to men £0.17.6 |
| | [1/8 each ie approx 8 pence] |
| *Total received* £22.10.0 | Fares from Oban £1.10.0 |
| | Telegrams etc. £0. 7.4 |
| | Carriage of gun from pier to hall £2.0.0 |
| | |
| *Cash in hand* £2.16.0 | *Total expended* £19.14.0 |
| | [approx. £3,000 today] |

The men travelled by train but their weapons were loaded aboard the Putter Dunlop, and shipped. Everyone seems to have had a pretty good time on less than a pound a head.

In response to rumours of a threatened invasion, the Volunteers had been raised in 1860 to defend Britain against the forces of Emperor Louis Napoleon. In the event, the French never did attempt an invasion and the need for the Volunteers scarcely existed. As an organ for uniting the men in a common enterprise however, the Volunteer company was ideal. It provided an excuse for getting together once a week and, like the Literary and Scientific Society, contributed hugely to the social life of the Slate Islands.

Amongst the long-standing members of the quarrying community Patrick had many friends from his schooldays. It grieved him to see these men and women fall upon hard times and he was always their champion in the many debates which were held in parish council meetings and on the pages of the *Oban Times*. In his capacity as justice of the peace he was called upon to write the occasional letter on behalf of the working classes who regarded him as a spokesman and man of letters. The following letter which Patrick wrote to the Marquis of Breadalbane, signed by Neil MacDougall, representing the quarry-men of Easdale Island, is one such example.

There had been an attempt by the company to make a charge for goods carried on the ferry between Ellenabeich and Easdale Island. Whereas custom had it that a person could transport anything he could carry onto the ferry unaided, free of charge, the company now wished to charge a penny for every package. For those living on an island where virtually everything in the way of food, fuel and household goods, had to be carried across on the ferry boat, this was an intolerable imposition.

On Patrick's advice, the men had petitioned the marquis with regard to this new ruling and His Lordship had responded by informing the company of the ancient ferry rules by which he expected the men to be governed. Despite the fact that the marquis had leased the quarries to the same company for a number of years, he, himself, held a considerable number of shares in the enterprise and still maintained sufficient influence to carry the day in any dispute over its management. The marquis had his agent, Peter Fisher, draw up a set of rules which he felt were fair to the men while meeting the obvious necessity of charging for exceptional loads carried on the ferry. The following copy letter in Patrick's own hand appears in his book for April 1894.

April 3rd 1894   Easdale
To the Most Noble, The Marquis of Breadalbane

My Lord Marquis,

Your general officer, Mr Peter Fisher, acting undoubtedly under your Lordship's instructions, supplied us with a copy of the proposed rules for the Easdale ferry. These were laid before a meeting of the quarriers and met with their approval.

The fact that our ancient privileges, the lengthened hours and the free carriage of all goods, have been maintained gives us deep satisfaction. I am instructed to reiterate all the previous expressions of our regard for Your Lordship's person and generosity and to express our gratitude for your timely intervention by which the matter has been amicably settled.

Your Lordship's most humble and obedient servant,

Neil MacDougall

Again, in his capacity of justice of the peace, Patrick took very seriously any criticism of the Law and the manner in which it was applied. Drunken brawls between quarrymen were not uncommon, the miscreants for the most part being taken into custody until they sobered up when they were usually charged with disturbing the peace. Generally a fine was imposed, sometimes a jail sentence. When a similar event occurred on Luing between one of the quarry managers and one Dr Black, the medical officer to the Luing Quarrying Company, no charges were made. Patrick wrote to the MP for the Lorn District of Argyll requesting a question be asked in the House.

Letter to Sir Donald MacFarlane MP
House of Commons London  31st July 1894

Sir,

I would feel very much obliged if you would ask the enclosed question in the House of Commons of the Lord Advocate. The question, which relates to a glaring and notorious miscarriage of justice, is a very needful one as this is not the first time in this district that a man in a good position has escaped punishment while justice to the very letter of the Law has been meted out to a poorer criminal. If the Procurator Fiscal and the police while possessing so much power are to exercise that power in an arbitrary and partial manner judicial justice will become a byword in this place and crime, instead of being suppressed, will receive tacit encouragement.

THE QUESTION
If, with the full knowledge of a serious assault and breach of the peace which occurred at Ballachuan, Seil near Easdale on the night of June 29th 1894, in which persons implicated, MacKenzie, slate quarrier of Port St. Mary, Luing and George Black, medical practitioner, Cullipool, whom did, while in a state of intoxication, grievously assault each other – the Procurator Fiscal for that part of Argyllshire was justified in suppressing the prosecution when other and comparatively trivial cases which happened about the same time, are brought to justice, whether the Procurator Fiscal has any right to consider the social position of criminals or to take into consideration petitions received from them.

The intention of this letter is quite clear even if the wording is somewhat convoluted. It was posted the following day but Patrick, having slept on the matter, must have changed his mind about its tenor because he followed it up with this telegram: 'IN ASKING QUESTION PLEASE DELETE NAMES OF PERSONS OMITTING ALL WORDS FROM "IMPLICATED" TO "WHOM DID, WHILE"'. Patrick was not looking for a libel suit as a result of his interference in the matter. He clearly felt an injustice had occurred, but was his protestation not coloured just a little by the fact that one of those implicated was his rival medic on Luing? Did he feel his medical colleague had let the side down, perhaps, or was he just exercising the antagonism he felt at the other's presence in the parish because Dr Black's practice must have reduced Patrick's own patient list quite considerably. Whatever his reasons, Patrick proved by this bold action that his leanings were without doubt towards the underdog at a time when others of his class still regarded working men as little better than animals and treated them as slave labour.

By April 1899 the plight of quarry workers was becoming desperate. Orders for roofing slates had fallen off, the labour intensive method used in their manufacture pricing Easdale slate out of the market; quarries were working only sporadically and the companies operating them were unable to meet their wage bills when pay-day came around, which was every six months. Patrick made some enquiries on behalf of the quarrymen concerning the effect of the Truck Act upon their general conditions of employment.

The Truck Act imposed upon employers of larger workforces the responsibility to provide a Company Store for the benefit of its employees. From this the employees could purchase all their household requirements. Employers took the Act as a licence to restrict all its employees' purchases to the company store. To go outside for supplies was cause for instant dismissal. Also, the Act gave the employer a free hand in the matter of charging for goods purchased and it was commonly accepted that these would cost more than on the open market. The reason given for the extra charges was that because the men were paid only once or twice a year they had to obtain credit in respect of goods purchased. Writing the amount owed on a slate which was kept above the counter became an accepted practice, and the commonly used term 'put it on the slate' entered the language.

The system had a certain additional benefit for the employer. Most of the families were in debt to the company store. Sometimes even after the half-yearly 'pay' had settled the most outstanding bills there was still something left on the slate. Since the men were unable to leave their employment before their debts had been cleared, the employers knew that they could rely on keeping a stable workforce.

It appears that the senior partners in the Luing Quarrying Company, J. and A. MacLean, took exception to Dr Gillies' continued interference in supporting the workforce against the owners. Citing the terms of the Truck Act, they had taken it upon themselves to appoint Dr Black as medical officer for their own quarries, a post for which Patrick had held the contract since 1893. Both Patrick himself and the Luing quarrymen who were his patients disagreed with this change, and the men contested their employer's right to appoint a new doctor without consulting them.

On 27 Apr 1899 Patrick wrote to Mr Kemp, a partner in the J. and A. McLean Quarrying Company which leased both the Balvicar and Luing quarries from Breadalbane. By letter, Patrick requested a copy of the agreement. It

The Cullipool Boys, employed in the Cullipool quarries c.1890. The manager is wearing a collar and tie. About a hundred men were employed on the island of Luing at any one time but the workforce was flexible, the quarrymen transferring if necessary to another island where production levels were higher. In periods of under employment some of the men would work small quarries on their own account and attempt to sell the slates made, either to the Company or privately around the district. Although Breadalbane generally

turned a blind eye to such activities, the sites chosen were rarely productive and the men barely scraped a living. Other unemployed quarrymen went fishing, stocking their larders with salted fish against the winter months when fresh food would be scarce. During longer slack periods, those without families emigrated to Canada, South America, South Africa, Australia and New Zealand. Around 30 men were employed on Belnahua, up to 200 on Seil and Luing and 100 on Easdale.

seems that Patrick's request was met by Mr Kemp because the following entry in the book is a handwritten copy of the form of agreement which had been entered into by the men and the quarrying company.

To the Manager, the Easdale Slate Quarrying Company Ltd in recognition of the Truck Act of 1831 and the amendment to the Truck Act (1887) and other Acts relating thereto:

We the undersigned hereby authorise you to deduct from the wages to be earned by us while in your employment, the amount of our house rent (should we occupy any house of which you are the owner or lessee) the sums to be paid by you on our behalf and the price of any fuel, powder, quarrying materials (including joinery work) tools or implements supplied to us and acknowledge that the above does not form a part of a condition of living.

    Date    Name    Address    Witness

This contract entered into between us and Messrs J and A McLean from this date until next pay-day at the rate of ------ shillings and ----- pence per thousand sizeables and -----shillings and ----- pence per thousand undersized slates made by us to be of the regulation size of 120 sq.inches. All slates made by us to be shipped by us according to the usual custom of the quarry. All medicines, medical attendance, fuel materials and implements to be deducted by the Quarry Masters at these contract prices.

From this Patrick understood that by signing the agreement, under the Truck Act the men had in no way authorised the Company to appoint a medical officer on their behalf. Since the men were determined to retain their rights in this matter, the disagreement continued and Patrick was ready to take the McLean brothers to court over his summary dismissal and the breaking of their contract.

However, a sharp letter from Patrick's solicitors pointing out the strength of Dr Gillies' case was sufficient to bring about Dr Black's dismissal without a court action being required. The partners had to agree that they had acted outside the terms of the Truck Act in employing Dr Black without the consent of the men and they could hardly argue with such a solid vote of confidence in Dr Gillies' favour. Reluctantly they were forced to accept him as their MO for a further four years, during which time Patrick refused to desist from involving himself with the workforce and their troubles with their employers.

The McLean brothers were later to meet with further resistance from the men resulting in a strike. The matter was fully reported in the *Oban Times* and, as the opinions flowed freely through the channel of this organ, Patrick himself was quick to take up the cudgels on behalf of his friends. The problem now was that the quarrymen at the Cullipool Quarry, in an attempt to

Men at work in the Balvicar quarries, c.1950, twenty years after Patrick's death. The method of working had not changed since the 1890s. While early in the twentieth century machines had been introduced to split the rock and cut it into roofing slates in the English quarries, Easdale slate was found to be too hard and blunted the saw blades.

At great depths below sea level, no matter how efficient the pumps, the quarry floor was inevitably wet, and the men were often obliged to work up to their knees in water. Wellington boots did not begin to appear until the end of the nineteenth century. Before this the men wore metal studied leather boots and heavy canvas gaiters, both of which failed to keep out the wet. The most common ailment of the quarrymen in Patrick's practice was rheumatism.

draw attention to the high-handed manner in which their masters were treating them, withdrew from that part of their working agreement involving the transportation and stowage of made slates in the holds of the sea-going vessels sent to transport them. In the past the men, who were paid per one thousand slates made, at intervals of six or twelve months, had accepted that included in the deal was loading the slates into the holds of the transports. In other words, the owners, instead of employing an additional force of stevedores, used the

A quarry worker drilling holes for charges prior to blasting slate rock from the quarry wall. The precarious perches on which quarriers worked were constructed of two iron rods hammered into the rock, upon which were balanced three wooden planks. A hand drill or mell of approximately 3 metres was forced into the rock at intervals to a depth suitable for blasting. Using a copper rod, black powder was tamped into each hole and a fuse, usually a series of straws filled with powder, was set to ignite the lot. The worker was hauled to the surface before the explosion occurred. A skilful quarrier could extract a neat cube of slate rock weighing several hundredweight which would be split into sheets and then cut into roofing slates of the required sizes.

quarrymen, thereby saving themselves a considerable sum of money. The quarrymen considered they should receive a share of this saving as payment for their efforts. The task demanded of them was far from easy. First the men must fill a small boat with slates, taking care not to damage them, for nothing was paid for broken slates. They then had to row the boat out into the Atlantic swell. While tossing about on the waves, they must carry the slates on board a larger vessel, stowing them carefully in the hold in such a way that they could not move on the voyage for the transport, whether bound for coastal towns in Britain or destinations as far away as America or New Zealand, would undoubtedly encounter rough seas and heavy weather.

Matters came to a head when the men refused to load the slates without additional payment. The McLeans refused to give in to such blackmail and instead recruited other men to do the loading. The Toberonochy quarry was failing and the men there had been on short time for many weeks. Without knowing the reason for their sudden good fortune, they were pleased to be offered the work. The McLeans, fearing a confrontation with the strikers, called in the constabulary from Oban to subdue any rising. When the Toberonochy men reached the outskirts of Cullipool village representatives of the Cullipool men met them and explained the nature of their argument with the company. The men from Toberonochy had no wish to be labelled blacklegs by men who were old friends, even members of the same family. They had their own grievances against the company and in better times would have joined the strikers. To the great disappointment of the small crowd of press reporters who had gathered hoping to witness a serious confrontation, they turned about and made their way home without even a harsh word having been exchanged. The McLeans, already humiliated by having to apologise to the police for calling them out without reason, were obliged to capitulate. The Cullipool men were promised additional payment for handling the slates, the amount to be agreed between the employers and the quarrymen's representatives.

Press reports of the incident gave various accounts of the happenings, their accuracy depending upon the moment at which a particular reporter had left the scene. Some had been in such a hurry to get to the telegraph office that they conjured up the expected conflict in the most lurid terms not realising that the matter had been resolved without any loss of blood. Consultation with any of the daily newspapers of the time leaves the reader in a state of confusion as to the outcome. Subsequent correspondence in the *Oban Times* however shows to what extent people were roused by the event, their opinions coloured by the daily paper they habitually took! This correspondence carried warnings of the rise of Socialism, the threat of strikes and the deposition of those whose natural birthright it was to rule over the masses. Although in the shipyards and coal-fields of the south it was true there was an amount of unrest being orchestrated by the trades unions, at Easdale the men merely wanted to get on with their work under acceptably safe conditions and to be paid regularly and fairly for their labours. When trades union representatives visited the district in 1900 they were given the cold shoulder, but instead of the employers showing their appreciation of this rebuttal by going some way to meet the demands of their men they did everything in their power to repress them. Admittedly, the slate trade was in a parlous state and the investors could see their dividends dwindling to almost nothing towards the end of the first decade of the twentieth century, but the company might have had a better chance of recovery if the employers had carried the men with them. Instead they now ruled over a disgruntled, disappointed and hungry workforce, with the brightest and best of the men leaving the area in droves to seek better lives overseas.

In 1906 the demand for slates had increased a little and there was some evidence to show that were another attempt to be made by a dedicated group of people, to open up a new quarry it might be possible to revive the industry in the district. Patrick and a small group of his friends decided to encourage the local quarrymen to get together to form their own company, taking the lease on a hitherto little-worked quarry on the Ardencaple estate called Carnan. Through his association with the Volunteers Patrick had made a good friend in Major Wilson, who was the commanding officer of the Easdale company and also, currently, the manager of Easdale Quarries. Unlike his counterparts the McLeans, Wilson had tried his best to give his workmen in the Easdale quarries the best conditions possible given the demands of his employers, the stockholders in the Easdale company. Wilson had agreed to support the efforts of those men, otherwise unemployed, who wanted to try their hand at self-employment. The men had no capital of their own, and it was Patrick Gillies who rallied financial support from sympathisers willing to lend money without expecting a dividend, on the understanding that the men would pay back the debt as and when profits allowed.

On 14 Jun 1906 Patrick wrote to Wilson, the quarry manager, concerning the lease he was negotiating on the Carnan quarry, opening with the following:

Dear Major

I had a long interview with Mr Robson yesterday and the position now stands as follows. He will do what he can to get the lease made over of twenty years with breaks at 5, 10, 15 years. The whole of the estate east of the breakwater to be marked off and no opposition allowed.

In addition to the area marked out for quarrying, the consortium was to lease twenty-five acres of agricultural land surrounding the new quarry. On this the men proposed to raise a maximum of ten cattle and fifty hogs. These could prove a valuable asset, particularly in the early years before the quarry went into full production. Patrick expresses some concern about his own liability in case the venture should fail. He is, however, satisfied that on the formation of a registered company this problem would be relieved.

Amongst his supporters Patrick included Mr Kemp, one-time partner in Luing Quarries but now, like the doctor, a sworn enemy of the McLean brothers. It appears Kemp had access to the slate market and also had a role in organising transport for the new quarry company as this letter from Patrick dated September 1906 suggests:

Dear Mr Kemp,

Many thanks for the extra shilling which I suppose you will stand to even if we do get a boat and as in any case we must cart wherever we go and it is not likely that the farmers will do it gratis this time, not in the midst of harvest! If you charter the 'Glendon', (Capt. Hamilton), you will find all right and he is coming with a cargo of coals to Buchanan at the next spring tide.

I hope you will pay for dispersing the 'fill' as every penny means much to these men. The rock looks extremely promising.

Yrs. Faithfully, Patrick H Gillies

'Fill' is the term applied to the waste slate and represents about 40% of all the slate quarried. This could either be used for 'metalling' pathways and roads or for infilling abandoned quarries. It always presented a problem of disposal but in this case, as Patrick had suggested in an earlier letter, the fill could be disposed of in the sea.

Kemp had found a buyer for the Ardencaple slate in Messrs Murray & Jamieson, a construction company in Edinburgh. Unfortunately, the terms of the agreement included a date by which the slates would be delivered. Because of inclement weather and a failure of the shipping company involved in the transaction, Patrick could see they were not going to be able to deliver the slates on time.

To Messrs Murray & Jamieson WS
Edinburgh                                                          Sept 10th 1906

Gentlemen,

We have made many efforts to get a boat to call for slates to Ardencaple but without
success. Should a boat manage to come into Caithlain creek to load and get safely
away the success of the quarry would be assured. We have at last got a shipper to
consent to try at the next spring tide, about the end of the month and should the
venture be successful we will at once let you know. With the present low price of
slates the necessity for carting them even a mile to a pier would reduce the profit of
working to nil besides causing considerable damage to the larger sizes of slates. I hope
therefore that you can delay completance of the agreement until this point is settled
when, should we be successful, every obstacle to the efficient working of the quarry
will be removed.

I am, Yours faithfully

Patrick H Gillies


Having at last found a ship, Patrick's troubles were still far from over. The
vessel sent had on board a load of coal to be delivered before it could collect
the slate.

Dear Mr Kemp                                                    18th Sept 1906

There seems to be a fatality about the quarry at Carnan. Shamkand, the Coal Merchant,
without Charles Buchanan's orders, sent the 'Bloodhound' instead of the 'Glendon'.
She has now to discharge 30 tons of coal in the creek and you might wire me on
receipt if we can load her. I suppose it is all right about the price as mentioned in my
last letter.
   With kind regards

Yrs. Sincerely

Patrick H Gillies


The unloading of coal in the creek having been successfully accomplished, the
slate was taken on board and Patrick was able to report to the buyers on 21 Sep
that the slate was on its way at last.

   The Edinburgh firm got its order eventually but it was quite clear that, however well intentioned, the new quarry at Carnan was unable to fulfil its orders
in a sufficiently professional manner to satisfy the contractors. As Patrick's letter
to Major Wilson of 27 Sep 1906 implies, Messrs Murray and Jamieson had no
intention of repeating their order. Nevertheless the men were determined to
carry on with the experiment and applied for a renewal of the lease, this time
for five years.

Dear Major

It is evident that we can expect nothing more from Edinburgh and it is the intention of the men to conclude the lease upon the present basis at the end of the month. They will I think, with a little help from outside, do well. We have got a boat to call right in to Caithlain; the Bloodhound of 100 tons taking a three quarter cargo from here. We are getting a boiler and engine next week and taking on half a dozen men. Can you undertake anything of our proposals in the circumstances?

With kind regards

Yours sincerely

Patrick H Gillies

Murray & Jamieson, having failed to obtain Easdale slate from any other quarter, were obliged to renew their order after all and on 11 Oct 1906 Patrick was writing to them with details of the next delivery and assurances that the men would be renewing their lease and in a position to supply further orders in the future:

Sirs

I am glad to be able to inform you that at last high tide the SS. Bloodhound passed through the creek hitherto described as non-navigable, drawing nine and one half feet of water. I am sure the men will be very glad to go with the lease in the circumstances. I will see them tomorrow and write for the documents thereafter.

Yrs faithfully, Patrick H Gillies

So convinced were the men now that their enterprise was going to succeed that they were prepared to invest in pumping and hauling equipment, essential if they were to continue digging down further below sea level. Patrick's next letter was to Mr Kemp for advice on the purchase of suitable equipment.

Dear Mr Kemp,

McKenzie and McDougall intend calling upon you tomorrow (Saturday) regarding the second hand engine etc. I hope you can arrange to give them easy terms even although you charge a little interest say to deduct so much from every cargo. This would give them a chance to get on. You might tell them of any likely places to see engines etc. I daresay it would be possible to get equipment landed at Ardencaple pier if not at the creek. There is no use their getting home an engine without seeing it personally as they will thus please themselves.

I hope you will do what you can for them in this matter of easy terms and if the slates suit you, I am sure they will not be likely to pass you.

Yours Sincerely,

Patrick H Gillies

On 20 Oct McKenzie and McDougall, two of the engineers who were part of the consortium of quarrymen, were in Glasgow negotiating the purchase of an engine and hoist. Patrick wrote to Kemp to ask him to negotiate terms for paying off the cost.

> Dear Mr Kemp,
>
> With regard to the purchase of machinery I do not see there can be much risk in getting it and deducting say £20 from each cargo. You did not find any risk in the case of the pump. They are men with a long lease of what is likely to be a profitable quarry and as little likely to fail in their engagements as others we know of. Surely this you could manage for them and if their slates are good the benefit could be mutual as you can have them at current rates, the profit would always be something.
>
> Yours very truly,
>
> Patrick H Gillies

Patrick had some problems with the solicitors drawing up the lease. Their failure to include a number of provisos and exemptions in the terms caused some of his prospective co-lessees to drop out. He now submitted the names of Norman Weir, proprietor of the Tigh an Truish Inn and Mr Samuel MacDougall of Oban Seil. Both gentlemen were known to Mr Robson, His Lordship's representative. Patrick begged that the final adjustment to the lease be made through his own solicitor in Oban, John M Campbell. He concluded his letter 'There is one point I hope you can give a definite promise upon and that is the letting of the park in which the quarry stands at agricultural value, to the quarry company at the termination of the present lease of Cammolaich Farm.' Ever the farmer at heart, Patrick could see how this additional asset might benefit the enterprise and occupy at least some of the men in leaner times.

Despite Patrick's efforts, Mr Kemp appears to have been less than co-operative in the matter of providing machinery on decent terms. At the end of October 1906 Patrick wrote to him again:

> I have seen Messrs MacDougall and McKenzie since they came back. It is a pity your quotations are so high but if needs must we can go in for a dear thing if it is thoroughly good and reliable. The terms are the difficult matter to arrange but if you could make it bills at 2, 4, 6 and 10 months in equal parts, I think we can get security good for ten times the amount. Please reply by return.
>
> Patrick H Gllies

Kemp must have found this proposed method of repayment satisfactory because on 18 Nov Patrick wrote to him:

If the following names will suit you to sign the bill along with McKenzie and MacDougall, you might let me know by return and send the bill and the matter will I think be concluded in a few days. I hope your firm will keep these matters strictly private as there are many roads leading to Easdale and its neighbourhood!

Names to sign:
　　　　　　　　Alan McKenzie
　　　　　　　　John MacDougall
　　　　　　　　Patrick H Gillies, Dunmore
　　　　　　　　Sam McDougall Inspector of the Poor
　　　　　　　　J McMaster Campbell Solicitor, Oban
　　　　　　　　William McPhail, Parish Minister

Meanwhile, Norman Weir, whose income derived solely from his position as landlord of the Tigh an Truish Hotel was getting cold feet. Should the Carnan Quarry project fail, he was likely to lose not only his investment but his livelihood as well. Having expressed his concerns and prevaricated for some time over concluding his own part in the deal, Weir received a letter from Patrick dated 8 Nov 1906. After a few polite preliminaries Patrick wrote:

> It is a great pity you did not consider the 'tread' dangerous when you pledged your word of honour to Sam [MacDougall] and myself. No one expects you to have knowledge of any 'tread' but one and that consciousness need not have bothered you.
>     When I spoke to you, you made one reservation only and that was that you must consult your lawyer. Even that you did not do as you had no time. I suppose Council matters and the letting of the Balvicar Road contract absorbed all your leisure. I do hope Colin and Donald Campbell were successful.

This last was a snide reference to Weir's involvement with the Council's scheme to improve the road across Seil. Weir held the lease on land from the Tigh an Truish Inn to the foreshore and anticipated a very considerable compensation payment to allow the road to pass in front of the inn. Colin and Donald Campbell were Weir's preferred contractors to carry out the work of constructing the road.

On 12 Nov 1906 Patrick wrote to Mr John Campbell, his solicitor in Oban, explaining that he had given Norman Weir 'a piece of his mind he will not forget' and concluding:

> I send you the draft lease for your perusal, if you find anything dangerous let me know. If not, you can just send it on to Tods, Murray and Jamieson naming the substitutes; the Rev. William McPhail for Weir and giving your own name. You may be assured that the chances of any payment falling upon us will be next to nil. I will write to Kemp today on the matter and the names on the bill will be McPhail, yourself and myself.

The gentlemen mentioned were trustees of the venture, whose cash investment was intended only as pump priming. They were to play no executive part in the scheme once the business was in profit. Patrick's involvement did not end here however. He was still concerned in the nitty-gritty of organising the new quarry. On 10 Nov he wrote to Kemp requiring half a ton of second-hand rails, an anvil and a Smithy hammer. Railway track was commonly laid in the quarries to facilitate the movement of slate rock and finished slates, the trucks being hauled about by horses and, by this date, small pug engines.

The arrangements were completed by 29 Jan and Patrick, in a letter to Kemp, explained that there would be a delivery of 85 tons of coal making up the bulk of the cargo. The equipment was duly delivered, but once installed it appears to have been less than satisfactory. On 15 Jan Patrick wrote to Kemp with a long list of deficiencies with both the boiler and engine which he had supplied. Kemp appears to have carried out the required repairs because in March 1907, Patrick wrote to the appropriate authority requesting information regarding the issue of a safety certificate.

25th March 1907

Dear Sir,

Carnon Slate Co.

In reference to your letters of 8th and 20th inst. I shall be pleased to know what is your rate for the inspection of the boiler which you have already tested and for the entry in the Register of the Exports and also if the test already effected fulfils the requirements of the Act for the next 14 months. I suppose it would be well to insure also but you might in the meantime let me have the above information.

Yours faithfully

Patrick H Gillies

This early form of today's 'Health and Safety at Work' legislation may not have been as stringent as we know it, but it was a long way from the days of the 7th Earl and his engineer John Whyte, when the safety of workers in the quarries lay solely in the hands of the proprietors.

By April 1907 word had got around that the workers' enterprise at Carnan was properly established and ready to fill orders for slates, on demand. This was one of many orders which Patrick was to acknowledge during the next few months.

Carnan Slate Quarry Isle of Seil                                    8th April 1907
To Chas. MacIntyre Esq. Land Agent and Architect Oban.

Dear Sir,

We are deeply obliged to you for your kind enquiry regarding Carnan Slates. We have over 20,000 on hand and would be able to supply a picked lot of the quantity you quire to Mr Jamieson. The price would be local and could be arranged later, say 72/- per thousand.

Yours faithfully, Patrick H Gillies

This is £3.60 in present values and a good price for the times, being worth about £540 per thousand slates today. During the 1860s slates were fetching only £1 per thousand. Today individual slates sell for up to £2 each! The price appears to have been satisfactory because on 30 Apr Patrick wrote again to MacIntyre's office, confirming that seven thousand five hundred slates would be delivered by the following Wednesday.

On 1 May 1907 Patrick had the satisfaction of sending MacIntyre a bill for £28 16s for eight thousand slates at 75s per thousand. On 4 May, however, he replied to a letter from Jamieson, a former client, who had indicated he would only pay 63s per thousand. 'We were not aware the price had fallen so seriously,' Patrick exclaimed. Things were beginning to look grim. The revised bill, sent on 4 May, is for 8,500 sizeable slates at 61s per thousand, the total amounting to £25 18s 6d. It seems a small enough drop by present-day standards but with large amounts still to pay off for equipment, the men were going to get a very small wage packet to take home to their wives.

After an initial period when the new quarry yielded high-quality slate the men began to complain of encountering poor rock with too many intrusions of the volcanic dolerite into the original slate beds. They found in addition an excessive amount of fissures and slipping in the seams which resulted in a very poor yield of the larger sizes of slates. Patrick, beginning to suspect that the venture was doomed to failure, was forced to write to the owners of the Ardencaple Estate, whose solicitors were Messrs Tods, Murray & Jamieson, with a request to terminate the lease on the ground where the Easdale men were quarrying.

It appears the Ardencaple Estate refused to cancel the lease, which was for a period of five years. The men must have struggled on, however, and perhaps found a benefactor to pay for opening a second quarry, for in 1911 they were still operating. In April of that year a Mr Wertheim, acting on behalf of the Easdale Quarry Company, contracted to buy from the Carnan quarry a load of slates in order to complete one of their own orders. The men set to with a will, spending the summer months preparing the slates. They were ready by the autumn and Werheim was invited to collect his order. The Carnan quarry-men were by now desperate for their money. Eagerly they awaited collection of the consignment of slates by Wernheim who had promised to remit payment at once. Having removed half the order, however, Wernheim's vessel was delayed by inclement weather and failed to turn up a second time to collect the remainder of the slates ordered. He had not yet paid for the slates he had already taken away.

Dec 1911

Dear Mr Wertheim,

I fully believed that you would have been able to implement your promises to pay promptly and regret to say I am now seriously inconvenienced thereby. I have already told you the reason I cannot, without great hardship, wait longer [ie that the men were dependent upon the money to feed their families]. If you however could send me £25.0.0 by return it would do in the meantime and the rest [of the shipment] could go in the fair weather after New Year. I will expect that amount by the end of the week and will write my banker in Oban to that effect as it is he who is pressing me in this matter.

Patrick H Gillies

Presumably the first consignment was eventually paid for, but in the new year there was a delay in collecting the remainder of the order and when the vessel at last came to take the slates away the men expressed themselves on the matter in very belligerent terms:

April 28th 1911

Dear Mr Wertheim,

I have just received your letter and gather from it that you know what took place yesterday. I think it is absolutely imperative for the sake of peace in the future that you fulfil absolutely and punctually, the definite promise contained in your letter to the clerk re-completion of payment on Saturday. It must be on Saturday and I can assure you that to delay it one hour will completely destroy in the men any respect they may still have for the word of the Easdale Slate Quarries Company in the matter of fulfilment of pledges. I think this would be deplorable and I rely upon you and honestly hope you understand the necessity for the utmost punctuality in the matter. The men are in a very suspicious state and in the face of what is going on in their quarries that cannot be wondered at. At any rate, should any failure to implement your written promise occur this time, you can never expect the services of anyone to intervene between yourself and them again.

I do trust you may be successful and speedily so, in getting affairs under way and I believe the men themselves appreciate your efforts but once again I say punctuality without any attempt at delay on this occasion will do more than anything I know to restore confidence and I hope that Saturday will see this matter brought to a satisfactory conclusion.

Having issued this very scathing criticism Patrick suddenly softens his tone, realising maybe that, whatever their feelings on the matter, the men might be dependent upon further orders from the Easdale Quarries in the future. He signs himself, 'With kind regards, Patrick H Gillies'.

By now it was not only the workers' co-operative at the Carnan Quarry that was in difficulties. The quarries on Luing and at Balvicar, leased by the McLeans, the Easdale Slate Quarrying Company in which Breadalbane himself still owned the majority of shares and the Belnahua quarries which were managed by the Shaws of Luing, were all in trouble. So too were the quarries at Ballachulish. A meeting, held at the estate offices at Kilmore, was called by Breadalbane in June 1911 to discuss the problems in the Scottish slate industry. It is indicative of the respect in which Patrick Gillies was held by the marquis, and indeed a measure of the friendship which had grown up between them over the years, that Patrick received this letter directly following the meeting.

Kinnel
Killin N.B.
June 3rd 1911

Dear Dr Gillies,

I was sorry I had not an opportunity of having a talk with you after the meeting yesterday [. . .] I thought I would like to explain to you the whole state of affairs. I was really sorry for the way in which the Rev. Malcolm MacCallum treated the whole matter today. I certainly think the way in which the Rev McPhail and yourself spoke is much more likely to get outside sympathy, and what we want is that something should be done to really benefit the district of Kilbrandon [rather] than the line adopted by the chairman of the Lorn District Committee. Of course you will kindly consider this letter strictly in confidence between us and as I have over and over again told you, any little thing that I can do in the way of helping the district I am willing and ready to lend a hand in.

Yours truly,

BREADALBANE

Breadalbane was right. Hand-cut slates were unable to compete in a market flooded by machine cut slates from England, Wales and places overseas such as Spain and Portugal. Although Wernheim tried to bring in mechanical saws to the Easdale quarries, they proved to be inoperable. The slate was too tough and quickly blunted the blades. Without doubt, the Easdale slates represented the better value for money: they have remained in the same condition in which they were first placed on the roofs of some of Scotland's oldest buildings for more than six hundred years. Imported slates such as those from Spain have a life expectancy of no more than thirty years. Those responsible for public building works however are inclined to go for the cheapest product knowing that any defects will probably not show up during the period of their own incumbency. They retire from office with a reputation for prudence and only several generations of councils later does the general public find itself footing another bill.

Patrick Gillies' adventure into the world of business and industry came to an abrupt end when the lease on Carnan Quarry expired towards the end of 1911. The consortium of quarrymen was in no position to renew it and, with the Scottish slate industry in such a parlous state, no benefactor was to be found who would invest in a further five-year tenancy. The quarries reverted to the landowners who continued to employ quarrymen from time to time to pro-duce small orders for local purposes.

The next three years saw a general diminution of the population of the parish as the men and their families drifted away to find alternative employment. This was halted only by the onset of hostilities in 1914 which meant that, although the men themselves went off to fight, the women and children were able to remain, sustained by their husband's army pay and by what work they were able to undertake in the absence of their menfolk.

The Carnan Quarry Company did not survive the First World War. Like those on Easdale Island and Belnahua, the Carnan quarries were abandoned when the men went off to fight. Left unattended, the deep pits filled with water. Any machinery which could find a market was sold off and the proceeds divided between the original investors. Few of the men ever returned to quarrying. At Cullipool, where the main quarry is above ground and not subject to flooding, operations were resumed in 1919, but subsequent slate production was inter-mittent and never reached the levels of former years. The Balvicar quarry con-tinued on a commercial basis well into the 1960s, when a major housing project to rebuild parts of Glasgow destroyed by bombing created a market for a short time. In the 1990s Angus Patterson, the last of the Easdale quarrymen, died and with him died also the last living recollection of a once noble industry.

# 12  Into Battle Again

THE YEARS IMMEDIATELY prior to the First World War were so eventful for Patrick in ways, both exhilarating and painful, that it is hardly surprising he made little or no reference in his records to what was taking place in the rest of the world at this time.

Events in the Balkans, the relationship between the British monarchy and its Russian and German cousins, even the outbreak of war in August 1914, two months after Hunter's death, went unrecorded by the good doctor. It was not until 1915 that Patrick finally woke up to the fact that his duties lay elsewhere. In a letter to Breadalbane's factor Mr Logan concerning matters related to the farm and dated 17 Apr 1915 he concludes with the following observation:

> I think there is an idea very strongly held just now and which is likely to take shape in the near future that the school medical service should be temporarily suspended and that the Medical Officers should help Civil Practitioners or get service in the RAMC. The matter was talked over in Glasgow on Wednesday at a meeting of my Committee and they are favourable and agreed to give leave.
> I think it is my duty as I have had training as an artillery officer and as an infantry officer and as during the Boer War I served in military hospitals, to serve my country in this emergency. I intend offering my services for the Royal Army Medical Corps and I hope I shall be accepted.
> My wife is quite agreeable. It will take some arranging here as I have taken a house in Edinburgh for the family during school sessions, but the fact of her being agreeable makes my duty plain and I hope the farm will not suffer in my absence. It is possible I may leave in two or three weeks.

In July 1915 he reported to Fort George and within three weeks was aboard the military transport ship *Bellaria* as Medical Officer in Charge of thirty-two

RAMC doctors, some two hundred orderlies and nurses as well as two thousand troops of various nationalities, bound for Gallipoli. As always Patrick kept meticulous records of his time on board, in the form of a daily journal.

The ship had been an ordinary cargo vessel but its holds had been hurriedly converted into sleeping accommodation for more than two thousand officers and men of the combined allied services. Narrow bunks had been constructed in tiers six high and in rows no more than two metres apart. The largest areas of accommodation in the ship, the officers' ward room and the seamen's mess, neither of which had been designed to accommodate more than twenty men, became the dispensary and the ship's hospital, while the original ship's hospital, a small cabin on the same deck, served as Patrick's office and living accommodation.

The ship's officers doubled up in their cabins to make way for the additional Army officers on board; the ship's captain occupied his sea cabin on the bridge, vacating his proper cabin for the use of senior Army officers Capt Graham, Royal Fusiliers, O.C. Troops and his adjutant Capt Tritona of the Dublin Fusiliers.

Patrick's instructions, given to him at Devonport by Major Powell RAMC and which he appended in his diary, were as follows:

1.  Conduct morning sick parade daily at an hour arranged in conjunction with the Officer Commanding.
2.  Make a sanitary inspection of the ship, daily.
3.  Hold a general health inspection within one day of embarkation and again one day before disembarkation.
4.  Transfer to hospital all serious cases occurring on voyage with Nominal Roll, Transfer Certificate and medical history sheet if available.
5.  Give a few simple lectures during voyage on community and personal hygiene.
6.  Attend to any cases requiring inoculation against typhoid and vaccination against smallpox.
7.  See paras 86-112 and 386 Regs. A.M.S. [Army Medical Service].
8.  At the end of the voyage hand over all medical equipment taking receipt to ship's purser or else to Military Authorities in the port.
9.  All unexpended articles such as sera, bandages, dressings etc. may be taken ashore with you to say, a military hospital.
10. Keep a record of all cases admitted to the hospital during the voyage.
11. Make particular note of all infectious cases or contacts.
12. In cases where there is no ship's surgeon on board you will be responsible for the health of the crew.
13. The telephone number in case of accident on board before leaving port is Devonport 152. Alternative, Central 52. Or if a personal enquiry Major Powell R.A.M.C, Devonport 420.

*Captain P.H. Gillies, RAMC, 1915.*

1st Argyll & Bute Artillery Volunteers, Easdale. The Volunteers were raised in 1860 at a time when Queen Victoria's regular army was thinly spread around the globe, busy helping to paint the map pink. There had been rumours of an intended invasion by the French emperor, Louis Napoleon, and it was felt necessary to defend our shores with local militia. The Easdale men were adept in the use of gunpowder and were considered suitable to train as an artillery company. They were also pretty handy with a sporting rifle when the Marquis' gillie turned his back. In the First World War a number of the Argyll Volunteers became members of the elite riflemen used as snipers in the trenches. Initially a battery of cannon dating from the Peninsular War was provided but these were gradually replaced by more up-to-date weapons from the Glasgow shipyards from the naval ships being dismantled or refurbished there. Forming the focus of social life on the islands, the Volunteers company was well supported by the quarrymen from 1860 until 1907 when the Territorial Army replaced it. The men took their training and duties very seriously attending camp annually and winning a number of prizes for both drill and shooting.

In his spare time Patrick was expected to oversee suitable forms of exercise for the men. These included Swedish Drill, the name given in 1915 to the exercises commonly used in physical education classes even today, deck quoits and all forms of competitive exercises of the kind with which he was already very familiar from his service with the Volunteers. During the voyage he instructed the troops in many aspects of personal health and hygiene while under fire, bringing to his discussion his own experiences in South Africa. His lectures also included such practical matters as the application of field dressings on the field of battle as well as the dangers of exposing oneself to venereal disease (with graphic accounts of the treatment involved and the dire consequences of not seeking such treatment).

It is clear from Major Powell's instructions that the Army did not have any idea what Patrick was likely to encounter once his ship reached its destination. There were no clear orders for him personally or indeed for the ship and its crew. It seemed to be a matter of 'get there, disembark the personnel and then do whatever they want you to, wherever you are needed'. As it was, the medical supplies remaining in Patrick's store when the ship arrived at the island of Limnos, which was to be a main base for the reception of casualties, were all he was to get with which to treat the hundreds of casualties that came on board as soon as the ship anchored off the beaches at Gallipoli.

The *Bellaria* left Devonport in the early hours of 13 Aug. Patrick at once constructed a roster of duties for his thirty-two medical officers and their orderlies so that the many medical functions to be performed could be shared equally between them. Hygiene was Patrick's first concern. Two thousand energetic young men performing whatever physical exercises could be devised for them and living in very close proximity to one another required to bathe frequently. Unfortunately the ordinary baths supplied slopped water over the sides as the ship rolled and the floor of the ablutions area soon became swamped. From the start Patrick had seen the problem and before leaving Devonport had demanded a supply of canvas baths that could be suspended like hammocks and would swing with the pitch and roll of the ship. They never materialised, and in the end it was the ingenious bosun who found the canvas and the men to make suitable baths for the soldiers' use.

During the first few days on board the medical staff had to attend to innumerable cases of seasickness. Without modern aids such as Stugeron and Quells, those who suffered from seasickness had to just ride it out and pray for calmer waters. As many of the medical staff also succumbed, it was left to those with the legs of old seadogs, Patrick amongst them, to clean up after the others.

It seems quite incredible by modern standards that such a large body of troops should have been allowed on board a ship bound for the Middle East without having received inoculations against typhoid and smallpox. Compulsory typhoid inoculation for troops had been introduced as recently as the outbreak of war in 1914 as a result of experiences of the South African campaign, while smallpox vaccination had been available since early in the nineteenth century so Patrick might well have assumed that most people on board carried immunity. Instead, he found that very few of the troops could provide evidence of immunity from either disease and he insisted that everyone else should get the needle. Those thirty-two medical officers were kept busy for the first week on board with this particular task.

The troops were on the whole fit young men just out of school, or they had come from Canada and other parts of the Empire where the privations of war had not yet made themselves felt. As might have been expected in such a large body of men there were some cases of venereal disease, which probably received better treatment here than they would have got had they never left home. For the most part, however, patients presenting themselves at sick parade had only minor problems: sore throats, ear ache, and other cold symptoms, and minor injuries caused by the pitching of the ship. There was, however, one suspected case of scabies.

Scabies is caused by the acarus, or scratch mite, which burrows into the skin and lays its eggs, causing at first a red patch and severe itching. Scratching on the part of the patient creates lesions in the skin which can become infected by bacteria. Scratching also spreads the mite eggs, via the finger nails, to other parts of the body. The lesions result in the eruption of septic pustules and subsequently the scabs of impetigo. If left untreated these sores may develop into septicaemia and render the patient quite useless for normal duties. The disease could not be allowed to spread throughout this large body of men living in such close proximity because it would seriously inhibit their ability as a fighting unit. Patrick took no chances.

The requirements of the treatment for scabies under wartime conditions are speed, efficiency and cheapness. In 1915 the only available application was sulphur. The patient was steeped in a hot bath for twenty minutes, lathered all over in soft soap and scrubbed in all affected areas with a nail brush. This was to open up the burrows of the acarus. The body was then rubbed all over with sulphur ointment. This part of the treatment was repeated every twelve hours until six applications had been made. After the last treatment the patient received a bath and his clothes and bedding were disinfected. One may imagine how relieved Patrick was to find that his single suspected case was a false alarm. It might well have become two thousand cases.

Shortly after leaving Gibraltar Private Morgan A. 19579, Royal Dublin Fusiliers, was admitted to the ship's hospital with obscure lung symptoms. As the patient was unable to spit he was not examined further for some hours until he had received several doses of expectorant. At last he was diagnosed with pulmonary tuberculosis and from then on kept under strict quarantine until the ship docked in Malta. Private Morgan was a very young recruit, probably no more than seventeen, and the encounter, so soon after Hunter's demise, must have been particularly poignant for Patrick.

Once the *Bellaria* had passed through the Strait of Gibraltar the doctors had another set of problems to contend with, these were related to sunstroke and sunburn. With so much time on their hands, the men had taken to basking on deck during the day, probably to make up for their disturbed nights below deck. Immediately, Patrick put out an order that no one should sleep on deck in daylight hours without wearing some kind of headgear and he reminded the men that in the Army, to allow oneself to become sunburned was a punishable offence. Unfortunately some of the many and various contingents on board responded to this order by ignoring it and Patrick was obliged on several occasions to draw their indifference to the attention of the CO Troops, Captain Graham.

> I again called the attention of the Adjutant to the necessity for orders being given to get the men to use a head covering when lying on deck. I brought before him a man whose face was badly burned from this practice. He issued orders to the (Military) police to see to the matter but as these orders were verbal I shall return to the matter tomorrow if proper instructions are not given in 'Orders' tonight.

An example of the haste with which the *Bellaria* had been provisioned made itself apparent to Patrick within days of sailing. Many of the drugs supplied had been delivered in cardboard containers instead of screw-topped jars. As a result many precious medicines which were deliquescent took up moisture from the increasingly humid atmosphere and were rendered useless. While this did not create problems on the voyage it was to cause Patrick much heartache when later he was obliged to treat wounded soldiers without the necessary drugs.

Shortly after leaving Gibraltar a man was brought to the dispensary at night, having had his forearm pierced by an iron hook. To his dismay Patrick found that the hospital cabin lights were not working and he was obliged to perform a minor operation by the light of a spirit lamp. Next day he ordered the steward to place a ship's lantern beside his bed to be ready for any other future nocturnal emergency.

When the ship arrived at Malta on 28 Aug a number of the medical personnel disembarked to take up posts in military hospitals on that island, which, because of its proximity to the fighting in Gallipoli, had become the main rear support for the treatment of wounded evacuated from the front. During the campaign the island was to become known as the Nurse of the Mediterranean.

Patrick went ashore in Malta only once, to receive his further orders and to attend a church service at the Presbyterian church on the island, conducted by one of the Army chaplains who had accompanied him aboard ship. His orders were to, 'remain on board ship in medical charge of the troops together with Lieut. W Doak RAMC and five other ranks. You will return to Malta on completion of duty.' Patrick spent the remainder of his time in port on board, requisitioning supplies which had been omitted in the provisioning at Devonport and trying to replace those drugs spoiled on the voyage. Among the requisitions were twenty suits of hospital clothing, three pounds of flowers of sulphur (other supplies having been used up in that non-case of scabies), a copy of King's *Regulations* (a War Office publication laying down the rules to be followed by serving Army officers in every circumstance), and two diary books. His journal so far had been written on Army communications forms. He also asked for a supply of quinine doses, the only remedy against malaria at that juncture. In his requisitioning he was only minimally successful because already supplies of many things were beginning to run out. Perhaps it should be pointed out here that had Patrick not had the experience of war in South Africa he might never have seen the necessity for these preparations. What was patently obvious was that there was no one on hand to tell him what would be needed in the days to come. On the other hand the lessons Patrick had given the troops on board the *Bellaria* should have stood them in good stead once they reached the squalid battle grounds of Gallipoli.

The ship sailed for Alexandria with only a small number of medical personnel on board and most of the two thousand troops. When she docked she disgorged her human cargo, to be quartered in training camps in Egypt before being sent up to the front. Only then did Patrick receive notification of the part he was expected to play in the conflict. He was to remain on board as senior medical officer in charge and oversee the conversion of the existing accommodation for use as a hospital ship. Experiences on the voyage had already alerted Patrick to the deficiencies of the living arrangements even for healthy young men. He now had to view what he had in the light of the wounded soldiers he could expect to be attending.

The two larger mess rooms, which had served as hospital and dispensary, were now converted into operating theatres, while the captain's accommodation became a ward for the most seriously wounded. The ship's crew continued to share their cabins watch and watch about and what remained of the medical staff arranged themselves in duty rosters in order to give twenty-four-hour cover. This had the effect of providing additional cabin accommodation, some of which could be allocated to the few nurses on board and also to the more seriously wounded officers.

Patrick viewed with horror the prospect of treating wounded men in the accommodation below deck. It was impossible to attend to serious casualties occupying bunks on the third tier and above, which meant that the majority of the available bunks could be occupied only by the walking wounded. Before leaving Alexandria Patrick must have considered having the top four tiers of bunks removed to give better circulation of air but time was against him.

Aware of the problems of maintaining high standards of hygiene on board ship, he had the bosun rig up additional latrines and ablution areas, and several more of the canvas baths were manufactured. The ship's carpenter was instructed to produce splints, crutches and other equipment likely to be of use. Patrick's efforts to track down and commandeer extra supplies of bandages and dressings together with the most basic of pharmaceuticals proved fruitless, and even such commodities as sheets and blankets were almost unobtainable.

The dietary requirements of wounded men differ from those of the healthy. At a time when refrigeration was in its infancy and certainly not a luxury to be enjoyed on *Bellaria*, the cooks had to rely upon dried and canned food-stuffs. The obvious choices of eggs, milk, fresh fish, fruit and vegetables for the patients were denied them. Powdered and canned milk and a form of dried egg, often suspect, and tinned meat prone to botulism, were all that was available. The one commodity on board which Patrick did not expect to find in short supply was water. As a steam ship the *Bellaria* manufactured its water supply by condensing the steam it produced for its own propulsion. At anchor, however, or when moored alongside in port, this function was very much reduced. When he set out with his newly converted hospital ship Patrick was not aware of this particular problem nor was he expecting to have the *Bellaria* anchored off shore for an extensive period. In less than a week Patrick's ship sailed for the island of Lemnos and from there to stand off shore from Suvla beach to receive the wounded.

The campaign in the Dardanelles had been in operation since April but very little news had been received from that front in England. What there was had been heavily censored, suppressed one supposes in order to disguise the fact that the whole operation was one of the worst disasters of the First World War. Whatever local research had taken place it was quite clear that the generals had either ignored the advice given by their spies or were so arrogant as to believe they knew better. They conducted a complicated invasion by sea with the minimum of planning, knowing little or nothing of the terrain the men would encounter once they were on shore. Perhaps more importantly, they underestimated both the tenacity and the fighting efficiency of the Turks, who were equipped with the most up-to-date weapons their German allies could supply. The Allied troops came under withering fire from the moment their transports neared the shore. Many died before they even got their feet wet. The beaches were not as wide, firm or gently sloped as the planners had been led to believe. When the lighters bringing the troops ashore had come in as close as they dared, the men leapt out into deep water and before they could struggle to land they were either shot or drowned.

The way off the beaches was by steep cliff paths which only men on foot and sure footed mules could manage and it was these animals which were to be the saving of those troops who managed to make it to the top and dig in. Under intense fire from Turkish snipers whose aim became legendry, men and mules kept up a continuous convoy of supplies, which included ammunition as well as sustenance to those fighting in the trenches.

The lack of water was a crucial factor throughout the campaign. Any reports concerning the lack of naturally occurring supplies in the area had clearly been ignored. In the event, every drop of water had to be carried ashore and up the cliffs by the mules. So much for Patrick's careful instruction to the men aboard the *Bellaria* concerning the importance of good hygiene while under fire. They had barely enough water to prepare their food and drinks, let alone to wash or shave themselves.

Despite his experiences during the Boer war, nothing could have prepared Patrick for the horrors which were about to fill his days. Situated as he was aboard the *Bellaria* as she lay in the roads off shore, he witnessed only the results of the battle, but these were enough for any man to bear. To understand the condition of the men brought to him for treatment we must turn to the first-hand accounts of those who survived the appalling and terrifying scenes on shore. Pte W. Begbie, Royal Munster Fusiliers, stationed on Cape Helles, recorded the following in his diary:

> When I fell for the second time I must have turned my arm because I found I was lying on my rifle with the butt about a foot from the front of my head. I was wondering what would be the best thing to do when I felt the rifle rocking and when I looked up I saw the butt had a piece of shrapnel embedded in it. I turned round and crawled back passing men of our company, some dead, and some obviously dying. Struggling to get my equipment off I heard voices then two first aid men came. They straightened me out and bound up my thigh. One of the men helped me to stand up, and with his help I was able to hop along the trench to the aid post. The MO said to the orderly. 'This man's dressing seems OK so if he thinks he can manage to hop to the wagons he can do so.'
>
> The ambulance wagons were well down the cart track the engineers had gouged in the bed of Gully Ravine and it led to Gully Beach where doctors and orderlies were working flat out to save the wounded who had managed to get so far, and many did not, for no stretcher-bearers could be spared to assist them. They had their hands full on the battle-field where the worst of the wounded lay helpless waiting for rescue, and those who could hop or stagger or crawl had to shift for themselves as best they could to reach the wagons that would take them to safety. It took them a long long time.

Pte Begbie goes on to describe how as the night wore on Gully Beach became an eerie sight, lit intermittently by the beams of searchlights reflected from the sky and by the glow of bobbing lanterns as orderlies moved among the wounded lying on the sand.

Other graphic descriptions, quoted in Arthur's *Forgotten Voices of the Great War*, were given of the flies encountered in the trenches:

> Millions and millions of flies. The whole of the side of the trench was one black swarming mass. Anything you opened, like a tin of bully, would be swarming with flies. If you were lucky enough to have a tin of jam and you opened it swarms went straight into it. They were all round your mouth and they got into any cuts or sores that you'd got which then turned septic.

One of the greatest scourges of the campaign was dysentery. As one Ordinary Seaman of the Royal Naval Division described it:

> Dysentry was a truly awful disease which could rob a man of the last vestiges of human dignity before it killed him. A couple of weeks before getting it, my old pal was as smart and upright as a guardsman. Yet after about ten days it was dreadful to see him crawling about, his trousers round his feet, his backside hanging out, his shirt soiled; everything soiled – he couldn't even walk.

The transports awaited by the wounded were no more than flat-bottomed boats used earlier in the campaign to land the horses. In the circumstances it is unlikely that these had received even a minimum of cleansing. The stretcher bearers were forced to wade up to their thighs in water as they transferred the wounded to the boats. Each boat carried no more than twelve stretchers at a time so progress was slow and although the movements continued throughout the hours of darkness the beach seemed no less crowded when daylight once again exposed the men to sniper attack from the surrounding cliffs.

At first, properly equipped hospital ships carried away the wounded to land them on the Aegean islands of Mudros and Limnos, lying some eighty miles to the west of Gallipoli, where field hospitals had been set up. Mudros was the Command Headquarters for the entire enterprise. It was a bleak barren island where even the General Staff occupied tented accommodation as did the field hospital. The field hospital on the nearby island of Mudros was provided with built accommodation for the hospital and received supplies of local produce to feed the patients. There was also plenty of water. Even here, however, the medical facility was quickly overwhelmed by the sheer numbers of casualties arriving daily.

Even at headquarters, supplies were limited by the delays in transporting materials by sea from Alexandria. As the numbers of casualties mounted the medical facilities ashore proved to be totally inadequate and the hospital ships, by now filled to capacity and running short of everything including food and water, were obliged to stand off until the men already ashore had either died or been moved on to Alexandria or Malta for treatment.

It was to this scene of chaos that ordinary transports such as the *Bellaria* were ordered, to take on the role of hospital ships. In some cases local boats, ferries and long-shore cargo vessels were commandeered or employed to remove the wounded. Without proper bunks, lacking dressings, bed pans or medical facilities of any kind, wounds quickly turned septic and many men died on board.

Although Patrick Gillies did not land at Gallipoli he was soon made very aware of these appalling conditions. From the moment she dropped anchor, the *Bellaria* was confronted by waves of casualties carried aboard from the lighters. The men were not only suffering from their wounds, horrendous as these proved to be: they were also undernourished, dehydrated, filthy and infested with every type of disease-carrying bug known to man! Of Patrick's patients, as many succumbed to dysentery, enteric fever and malaria as died from their battle wounds.

Understaffed, with very limited equipment and lacking the barest essentials such as dressings and disinfectants, Patrick laboured to save the lives of those who could be saved and to make comfortable those who could not survive for more than a few hours. Having taken on board as many of the wounded as the ship could carry the *Bellaria* sailed for Limnos, only to be told on arrival that she could not disembark her casualties. Patrick was furious and went ashore to demand proper accommodation for his patients. What he found there convinced him that they stood a better chance by remaining on board the *Bellaria*. Instead of waiting around until sufficient space could be found at the base hospital, he asked the captain to sail for Alexandria. During the next few weeks the *Bellaria* returned several times to Gallipoli, collecting casualties and delivering them to Alexandria. Eventually Patrick received orders to transfer to the hospital ship *Letitia*, where facilities were more appropriate but the injuries confronting him no less horrific.

The withdrawal from the heights of Gallipoli began just after Christmas 1915. One man of the Royal Marine Light Infantry described how his company awoke one morning to find that the French trenches next door had been deserted. The British Royal Marines were ordered to spread out into them to give the Turks the impression that the Allied numbers were still the same. When the order came at last for them to withdraw, the marines found that both Anzac and Suvla beaches had already been evacuated and that in fact they were the last of the Allied forces to be occupying the sector. Even as they packed into the lighter which was to ferry them to safety, *Asiatic Annie*, the great gun mounted on the headland, which had continuously harassed the Allied forces for many months, was still firing her shells at the departing British soldiers. Also, towards the end of the year, orders came through for Patrick to join the staff of the military hospital at Ghain Tappertia, Malta as the MO in charge.

In March 1915 Malta had been formally declared a base hospital although the entire island was only equipped to cater for a few hundred patients. By March 1916 there were twenty thousand convalescent soldiers on the island, the first convoy, of some six hundred wounded from the Dardanelles, having arrived in May 1915. Twenty-seven hospitals and convalescent camps were set up using public and private buildings, including schools which had been converted for the purpose. During the whole war period about eighty thousand wounded and sick officers and men were cared for in Malta, including some twenty thousand from the Australian Expeditionary Force.

St Andrew's Hospital at Ghain Tappertia was a convent and hospital, very well run by experienced nuns. At last Patrick was able to practise his skills in surroundings which provided assurance that some at least of his patients stood a chance of recovery from their wounds. Unfortunately, this improvement in circumstances came too late for Patrick himself. Overworked aboard understaffed hospital ships, he had been exposed day by day to every kind of medical as well as surgical affliction. Unable to take proper care of his own personal well-being, he at last succumbed to dysentery himself and although nursed back to health by the sisters he was too weak to carry on. As soon as he was well enough to make the long journey home by sea, he was transferred to the home front. A period of recuperation was followed by an appointment to the Ministry of National Service, and, much to Mary's relief, he found himself stationed in Edinburgh.

# 13 Aftermath

O N HIS RECOVERY from the effects of his tour in the Middle East, Patrick was posted to the Ministry of National Service in Edinburgh where, in the summer of 1916 he took on a role as a district MO, taking charge of the physical examination of recruits and also sitting on the appeal boards of those claiming exemption from call-up. At this stage in the war the men called up for service were either very young or well over the normal age for call-up. Some youngsters he suspected of being no more than fifteen. The middle-aged men were in the main those who had been passed over in the early days of conscription for minor physical defects or because of their family commitments. By 1916, however, such niceties were no longer observed. The ruthless war machine demanded more and more cannon fodder and everyone, able-bodied or not, was called into the fray. Having seen what became of men who, after only a few short weeks of training, were placed in the firing line, Patrick must have had many misgivings about declaring them fit for duty.

The offices to which he reported were in the Adelphi Hotel in Cockburn Street, Edinburgh, just a short distance from the family's temporary home at Hartington Gardens. Patrick was, for a time, able to live at home and to see something of his growing family. Alexander, in the sixth form at Watson's was anxiously awaiting call up, while Hugh and the youngest son, Jackie, were still in the lower school. The Dunmore farm was under temporary management for the duration and tenants had been found to occupy Ballachuan. When an opportunity arose during school holidays, the whole family would take a few days to visit their newly acquired house at Connel into which Patrick and Mary had moved in 1914, following Hunter's death. This more comfortable life lasted for most of the year 1917, but then Patrick was moved again, this time to Nairn in Invernesshire. Mary remained in Edinburgh keeping house for her three schoolboys.

Early in 1918 Mary's brief respite from anxiety ended. Having reached his eighteenth birthday Cammie enlisted and, following the Easdale Volunteers' tradition, joined the Royal Artillery. As a pupil at Watson's Academy he had served in the Officer Training Corps (OTC) so by October 1918 he was already undertaking initial training at the officer cadet school at the Preston Barracks of the Royal Regiment of Artillery at Brighton in Sussex. Cammie's correspondence indicates that Patrick had been transferred to London for a spell, possibly between postings.

Mary must have dreaded the day her son passed out from the officer training school while Patrick's feelings on the matter can hardly be imagined. Within a month of his receiving Cammie's letter, however, the armistice had been signed and the threat to yet another of their boys averted. Cammie was discharged in order to take up his medical studies at Edinburgh University never having fired a shot in anger, while Patrick moved to Nairn, and his job, which had been the medical inspection of recruits to the armed services, changed to one of assessing the degree of disability of pension claimants. He was promoted to the post of District Medical Officer Commanding the North East Region.

The organisational features of his work, both with the Ministry of National Service and the Ministry of Pensions differed little from that which Patrick had set up for himself in order to examine school children in Argyll. With a couple of orderlies to replace his school nurse, he now toured the Highlands with all the accoutrements of a medical examinations centre: screens, scales, medical instruments and testing apparatus for eyesight and hearing. All was loaded onto whatever form of transport could be commandeered. To begin with, the scheduling of these tours was done by clerks in the head office of the ministry, men with little or no comprehension of the transport facilities available in the Highlands. Their enquiries informed them that ferries existed between islands and that trains or buses ran between certain centres of population, but their schedules made no allowance for such facts as ferries that ran on Tuesdays and Thursdays only and buses whose arrivals did not correlate with train departures.

October 1st 1918

The Orkney tour was arranged with a view to leaving Orkney for the mainland on completion of the Stromness Board. The decision for the party to go on to Shetland was known only after the arrangements for Orkney had been made. Kirkwall should actually have been done last on the list as it is little over a mile from Scapa. As it is one must make the best of it [. . .] just another administrative muddle!

Patrick was meticulous in keeping a record of his movements day by day and of his expenditure on travel and accommodation. His diary for 1919 tells a story of the constant frustrations he encountered: hours spent waiting on station platforms, days waiting for the next ferry. There were instances of his team arriving in small out-of-the-way places to find no suitable accommodation either for the MO or his men. In this year he travelled to Thurso and took a ferry to Stromness in Orkney where he had to hire, at considerable expense, a rickety old car to drive him to the various centres on that island. The vehicle was not equipped with luggage space suitable for the equipment they carried so the two orderlies were obliged to travel by horse and cart, making the interviews a day late in starting. On another occasion he was obliged to take a taxi all the way from Thurso to Ullapool because there was no form of public transport available. Patrick's correspondence for the period contains many letters to head office in answer to some clerk's request for an explanation for exceptional expenditure on transport and accommodation.

The clerks occasionally made even worse errors when summoning pension claimants to these examinations boards. In one instance a man who had lost a leg at the Somme was directed to present himself for examination at Stromness on a particular date. His journey by sea and overland from one of the more remote islands took nearly a week. By the time he arrived, the board had moved on to a different location. As Patrick's report argued, the man had lost a limb, about this there was no argument. It was obvious that he was due compensation so why had he been called for examination in the first place?

Ever the pragmatist, Patrick ensured that each time some mishap occurred he recorded the local solution, keeping careful note of timetables and means of transfer from one centre to the next so that he was able eventually to compile quite different schedules which would work in the future, both for himself and anyone else who followed. What he had not reckoned with however was the petty jealousies and the stupid rivalries which existed between the regular Army officers in command and the medical officers working in the field. It was more important apparently that a senior man's decisions be unquestioningly upheld than that a practical solution be applied to a problem. It appears that Patrick should have waited, no matter for how many days, for the transport arranged by his superior, rather than proceed under his own initiative. The Army always paid up in the end but the letters exchanged between the doctor and his CO became more and more acrimonious as time went on.

Disputes also arose concerning what Patrick and his colleagues considered to be a legitimate claim for compensation from some of the ex-servicemen. Head Office was very quick to question too long a list of men recommended for a pension. In a number of cases Patrick was accused of giving a too gener-ous assessment of a man's disability. At the same time, he himself queried the results of boards held by his colleagues: not all the military doctors engaged in this work were as sympathetic to the disabled as was their director. On the second of February 1917 the District Administrative Officer, R.G. Geddes, complained to Patrick's immediate superior:

Dear General Culling

Capt. Gillies is making a great hash of the proceedings of boards held under Regs 1199/17 which he frequently returns to the presidents for correction when they are quite in order. He charges the members with carelessness in working out the proceedings when it is his own lack of intelligence that is at fault. As he writes in your name I can't very well get at him and I therefore write privately to ask that you instruct him to learn over and over lines 19.10 and 16 of ACI 1199 A4 930, until he can repeat them to you by heart. It is only four lines and that should not take him more than an hour! I hope after that we shall not have so much correspondence about transfers to Class W.

I hope also for some improvement in Capt. Gillies' epistolary style which is not always as courteous as it might be when addressing this officer in your name.

Yours sincerely,

RG Geddes ADMS East District, Perth

At each location, Patrick was required to set up a board consisting of two local doctors and himself to examine the cases of men claiming compensation for war wounds, seeking to enlist or trying to avoid the call-up. What the ministry clerks had failed to recognise was that because so many doctors had been called away for war service frequently one general practitioner was holding the fort for two or three others, and, with his general duties trebled, the doctor had no time to spare for Patrick's examination boards. Again Patrick found his actions in question when from time to time he was obliged to hold a board consisting of just himself and one other. On one occasion he had to perform the examination alone as the other doctor appointed was obliged to answer an emergency call at the last minute.

Not all the local men were up to the job as Patrick records after his visit to Stromness on Orkney.

October 2nd 1918
Board at Stromness
Members     Dr Heddle (Kirkwall)
                 Dr Petrie (Stromness)

Petrie turned up fairly drunk but quiet. I made him President of the board and installed him in the chair where he sat looking very wise. If he were not so well known to all present, including the recruits no doubt, he would have made a very dignified figure. He had had a big bout the day before so he was in a more or less stuporous state.

Setbacks such as this led Patrick to query the efficacy of engaging local practitioners at all in the work but under no circumstances was the Army going to send a team of three doctors around the countryside to examine the small numbers of men summoned to meet the board. Another bone of contention was that having travelled, usually in some discomfort, great distances with his two orderlies and all their paraphernalia, Patrick often found an initial list of, say, a dozen men had been reduced to one or two by the time they arrived. The reasons for these absences were usually quite legitimate. Sometimes the applicants had died while waiting for assessment of their wounds or had made such a recovery as to feel the board unwarranted and head office had failed to notify Patrick of the changes before he set out. In cases of recruitment examinations, however, the inconsistencies lay squarely at the door of the office staff. On 2 Oct 1918 Patrick was in Stromness where he recorded:

Of the twelve men who turned up at the Recruiting Board three were Northern Lights men [lighthouse keepers, exempt from call-up] who came voluntarily. Another who was voluntary came only because he wanted grading for his own satisfaction. A fifth had been called up by Aberdeen leaving only seven called by Inverness. A disgraceful state of affairs . . . a medical board to be sent north for such a small number! The Registrations Department is to blame I suppose, but there is something very wrong in it all. The want of a local man in the outlying districts is another drawback to efficiency.

Men were occasionally scheduled for examination who had already signed on long since and were already enlisted and in training camp, and, particularly in the case of the Hebridean Islands, men who had been quite legitimately serving all through the war as merchant seamen had been recorded as avoiding enlistment and summoned to attend a recruitment board. Patrick, who had many friends in Argyll who were merchant seamen, found this type of error particularly offensive and was quick to remonstrate with his superiors over the matter.

Sometimes the difficulty of finding suitable members for a board was solved by one of the doctors on central office staff themselves joining Patrick. This they undertook willingly, particularly in the summer months when a short trip through the Highlands seemed preferable to spending one's working hours cooped up in a stuffy office in Edinburgh. On these occasions Patrick would put himself out to ensure that his travelling companion, generally a gentleman of higher rank than himself, was properly accommodated and that the travel arrangements went as smoothly as he could manage. Unfortunately the officers in question did not always decide to accompany him until the very last minute and sometimes they did not turn up at all. This of course made his arrangements much more difficult. During the years 1918 to 1920 Patrick was to experience many incidents of this kind and had become almost inured to the casual treatment he received at the hands of his colleagues. In August 1920 however, a certain Dr Lyall, who had applied to accompany Patrick on a trip to Wick and the Outer Hebrides had not confirmed his time of arrival, so Patrick's clerk in the Inverness office took the liberty of telephoning headquarters to enquire of Dr Lyall's intentions. This innocent query was to trigger a series of acrimonious correspondence which had a drastic effect upon Patrick's future. On the 31 Aug 1920 the following letter was received at Patrick's office in Inverness from the Ministry of Pensions Headquarters, Scotland Region:

Adephi Hotel, Cockburn Street
Edinburgh.

To Dr Gillies
Ministry of Pensions
7 Baron Taylor Street, Inverness

My Dear Gillies,

A telephone message has just been received in this office asking whether Dr Leslie Lyall will be available for out-station boards in the Northern Area. Dr Leslie Lyall will not be available for these boards neither will any other DCMS at Regional Headquarters. This telephone message is not understood. The Board work in the Northern Area has been recently arranged so that you have much less travelling than you used to have. Instead of going around the Outer Isles about five times a year you now go either once or twice, and the same should apply to every part of your area. There has been plenty of time during the past eighteen months to arrange the work in your area so that you should be able to undertake it without assistance from the DCMS at Regional Headquarters. The other DCsMS in the Scotland Region do not require to have DCsMS from Regional Headquarters to assist them.

Please let me know what you have done about your holiday and how much of it you had and let me know what arrangements you are making about it so that it will not interfere with the board work in your Area. I think of course that the telephone message is a misunderstanding by the clerks in your office during your absence but I would like to know as soon as possible what arrangements you are making that the board work in your area is being kept up to date without assistance from Regional Headquarters.

Yours sincerely George Gibson

Gillies, who was away at the time on another tour, received a copy of this letter together with a note from his clerk, A.G. Wallis, dated 2 Sep 1920.

Dear Dr Gillies,

I opened the enclosed which came addressed to you under confidential cover. It is perhaps as well I did so as I was just going to ring up headquarters re Dundee DCMS as per your wire! The phone message in question was one I put through to ask Dr Lyall if he was going to Wick. I wrote him on 26/8/20 as I advised you, but had got no answer and as the time was getting on I rang up to see and as he wasn't in I left a message with Dr Hodgson. I still had no word and rang up again the result of which I wired to you to say Dr Lyall was unable to go.

The CMS letter is most unreasonable but I think if you remember incidents in the last journey to Orkney we may be able to arrive at a good idea of the cause of the trouble. The whole thing is a little sickening and I wish I was out of it. In the meantime I have made no arrangements for the Hebrides Board and cannot now do so pending your instructions. I have wired you to say I am sending on this letter.

Yours faithfully, A G Wallis

Patrick was incensed by the implication that either he or his office was under-performing and wrote the following reply on 7 Sep 1920:

Dear Dr Gibson,

I received your confidential letter of 31st August on my arrival here yesterday from Coll and Tiree.

I regret that any misunderstanding should have arisen in the matter of employing DCsMS Headquarters [staff] on out-station boards but on no occasion (except that on which Dr Keely acted during my illness, was a DCMS other than myself necessary for work in the Northern Area. On no occasion did I ask for their services and on the present occasion as on past occasions, the initiative came from your headquarters and not from me. On every occasion the journey and the itinerary were made to suit their convenience not mine. In the future you may rest assured no more cheap holidays or sight seeing will be arranged for them by me except on your direct instructions.

I am sorry to say that I was under the impression you were quite cognisant of the position. I may point out that on many occasions I offered to do the work myself and in one particular case, was deliberately employed elsewhere in the Scottish Region while your DCMS toured in the West. These are facts somewhat inconsistent with the spirit of the first paragraph of you letter.

With regard to holidays, the delay in receiving necessary documents from Regional Headquarters forced me to forgo my prearranged leave in July. At the last moment with numbers incomplete I was instructed to proceed with Mull, Coll and Tiree, so that again, my leave had to be postponed. Before leaving for the west I phoned Dr Buchanan and agreed to hurry up the examination of Mull, Coll and Tiree pensions and arrange three weeks leave after that.

I finish with Mull tomorrow afternoon and intend to take 20 days leave beginning with Sept. 9th. The balance I can settle for again.

In consequence of your letter I am making arrangements for the Outer Isles Board to be postponed a week and will draft a programme of all the Island Boards to run consecutively thereafter.

Yours sincerely, Patrick H Gillies

PS I expect to be here for a few days.

After a night's sleep he felt no better about the situation and on 8 Sep penned the following letter of resignation.

To the Secretary of Military Service, Adelphi Hotel, Cockburn Street, Edinburgh

Sir,

On further consideration I think the spirit of your letter of the 31st ult., so utterly unjust that I have no desire to continue in the service of the Ministry of Pensions. I herewith give you a month's notice of the termination of my employment and will thank you to acknowledge receipt to Headquarters Inverness Area. I am sending a similar notice direct to the Ministry of Pensions, London.

It may have been a hot-headed decision but it was clear from the diary of his journey the previous year through Orkney and Shetland that Patrick was tiring of the petty officials and the bureaucratic muddle in which he was expected to operate. There is little doubt that he was looking for an opportunity to get back to a more regular life centred on his own home. His colleagues however were far from complacent about his resignation.

Gibson, realising he had gone too far, attempted to rectify matters in a letter to Gillies dated 10 Sep 1920.

Balmoral Hotel
Edinburgh

Dear Gillies,

I was very sorry to get your letter and also the official note you sent tendering your resignation. As to your statement of injustice that to me is the worst blow you could give me and to me the greatest sign of failure on my part. The last thing I would wish is that you should resign. I think that before doing so you might come here and discuss the question with me. Second thoughts are frequently best. If after seeing me and talking over the question dispassionately you still wish to leave, nothing more can be done.

During this month I am to be in the office every Thursday and Friday so would be grateful if you will come and see me. Meantime I am holding your letters –

Yours sincerely, George Gibson

But Patrick had already side-stepped his boss and gone straight to the ministry in London.

Ministry of Pensions,
5, Millbank, Westminster, London

Sir,

I have the honour to notify you of my intention to desist office as Deputy Commissioner of Medical Services under your ministry my resignation to take effect on the 8th October 1920.

Please accept this as the statutory month's notice and acknowledge receipt to the above address.

I have the honour to be your most obedient servant

Patrick H Gillies

Note: I have sent a similar communication to the secretary of Medical Services Ministry of Pensions, Edinburgh.

Mavericks like Dr Gillies were disturbing to have around but Gibson was forced to admit that Patrick had managed to get things done in a way that many others had failed to do. Recognising that he was losing a valuable member of his staff he was open-minded enough to acknowledge Patrick's contribution to the service.

Balmoral Hotel
Edinburgh
21.9.1920

My Dear Gillies

I have just received your letter and wish to thank you for it. I am sorry that you do not wish to withdraw your resignation as we can ill spare you in the North and West. I cannot see that we will get anyone to run the show as well as you did. However you seem to have definitely decided so that we must look for someone to take your place.

The DCMS have not given me an idea of the question. I quite understand that they were not helping at your request but in order to assist in carrying out investigations concerning the particular specialities. The mistake was mine in taking a telephone message I got as an official communication and writing as I did to you.

I wish to thank you for the way you have always administered the Northern Area and the highly efficient manner in which the boards have always been conducted. Your advice regarding local conditions and the excellent relations you maintained with the medical men in the North have been of the greatest possible assistance. I am extremely sorry to see you go …

Could you please submit a formal letter of resignation which I can forward to London.

Kind regards and many thanks

Yours very sincerely

J Gibson

Patrick too, clearly hoped to pour oil on troubled waters when he replied from his Easdale residence while taking a few days well-earned leave:

Ballachuan, Balvicar by Oban, Argyll.

Dear Dr Gibson,

I only received your letter on Friday last. It had been returned to Inverness by the Ministry people and then forwarded here.

I regret very much that the wording of my resignation should have annoyed you and I unreservedly withdraw the imputation of injustice on your part which it conveyed. At the same time I feel that the DCMS, who have availed themselves of the opportunities which journeying in the north offered and which I took much trouble to help them to, have not been fair in the matter and I must conclude that they gave you the impression that they were helping me at my request. The facts of the case are as I stated in my letter and I would like you to know if my conclusion is correct that I am very sorry for any expression of mine which may have caused you pain or annoyance.

Regarding my resignation it was exceedingly kind of you to suggest withdrawal. That, I am afraid is impossible now. In a short time I should have been in any case at the parting of the ways and I have now definitely fixed to return to my County work here. I leave my work with keen regret. My heart was truly with the Highland people for I love them and their ways and were I not a professional man, I too should be a sunyiefeiner [Gaelic: one who can always find an excuse to put things off until the last minute] so perhaps you are well rid of me.

May I in conclusion express my thanks to you personally for your kindly forbearance in dealing with the problems of command in the North. I felt that you understood the position and really had pleasure in carrying out my duties under your direction. I can honestly say that I enjoyed my work very much.

Yours very sincerely,

Patrick H Gillies

Not only at odds with his bosses over the beaurocracy surrounding his work, Patrick was disgusted at the indifference of those in charge to the plight of wounded ex-servicemen and their families. On 4 Jan 1919 he visited the island of Coll intending to assess the condition of a pensioner called John McLeod. He found that the man had died the previous October from the debilitating effects of tuberculosis, contracted in the trenches and exacerbated by dysentery. His wife had nursed him for many months and when he died, as Patrick was to point out in his report, 'all clothes, bedding etc. were burned to prevent infection and she got no compensation as she had not first got the sanction of the Sanitary Authorities. The widow took to her bed and has not been up since. She looked very thin and anaemic. She gets no pension.' It is hardly surprising that Patrick left the Ministry of Pensions feeling that his time had been wasted and his work unappreciated.

Patrick's immediate concern now was to secure a position in civilian life commensurate with his current status. Having tasted the fruits of life as a local-government servant and apparently undeterred by his unfortunate experiences with military administration he appears to have rejected any idea of returning to his former practice at Easdale. He began to make enquiries amongst some of his more influential colleagues. Many of his senior officers thought highly of Patrick's efforts to overcome the log-jam created by War Office beaurocracy and gave him glowing testimonials on his departure. His immediate superior, Dr Mackay of the Inverness office, arranged an interview for him with Sir Leslie MacKenzie who held a position of some importance in the realms of local administration.

Dear Mackay,

Tell Dr Gillies that I shall be delighted to see him when he calls. I cannot fix an hour but he should just take his chance and call [. . .] Norman Walker confirmed in advance all you say. It was he I think that appointed him to the pensions post. He spoke of him in the highest terms and said to me that he was a man to keep in view. A man that impresses two people as different as Walker and yourself must be made of the genuine stuff! I have seen him once but I am not sure if I have even shaken hands with him.

As it happened, Sir Leslie's intervention in Patrick's job seeking proved unnecessary. Quite fortuitously Argyll County Council had at their last meeting agreed to restart the schools medical examinations programme and Patrick was invited to re-assume his former position. Ambitious man that he was, he returned to the fold knowing full well that the chief medical officer for the county, Dr Mac-Neill, whom he respected greatly, was already past retirement age. Indeed, had it not been for the fact that so many men had been killed in the war and there had been a general suspension of the normal retirement age in order to make up for the shortfall in the council's staff, Dr MacNeill would have been long gone. Unfortunately for Patrick there was still no pressure upon MacNeill to resign and he was to remain in post a further four years, until his death in 1924.

From the comfort of Manee, the Gillies' new home in Connel, Patrick returned to the medical inspection of school children in Argyll in time for the autumn school term. In his diary for 1919 he had recorded with some satisfaction that he had at last been able to give up the lease on Ballachuan to a new tenant, while Dunmore remained in the capable hands of his farm manager. The income from the farm must have been a help at a time when he was between jobs but he was quite clearly anxious to be rid of the responsibility and delighted when, the lease having at last run out, he was able to withdraw from the Dunmore estate with a sizeable sum raised from the sale of stock and farm equipment. Cammie was by this time at university, engaged in his medical studies, while the younger boys, Hugh and Jackie, still at Watson's School, continued to be a drain on his finances.

During the five years in which the medical examination of school children had been in abeyance a whole generation had passed through the system and Patrick was obliged to start again from the beginning, seeing only school leavers at thirteen and new entrants at age five, together with those individuals brought especially to his attention by the teachers. To his dismay he was to find an increase in the number of such 'special' cases. The war had stripped many families of a breadwinner while others found themselves burdened by fathers returned as helpless invalids, either physically or mentally. Patrick was confronted not only with poorly clothed and malnourished children but also, sadly, those who for what ever reason had been severely abused by their parents. Each of these, in his or her own way, was a casualty of war.

# 14 Sixty Seconds' Worth of Distance Run . . .

A LTHOUGH DURING THE later stages of the war the medical inspection of school children had been officially suspended, from the time of Patrick's departure in 1915 until July 1916 the school nurse, Miss Simpson, continued to make the rounds, recording weights and heights, inspecting the children for infestations and reporting to the Local Authority upon any outstanding cases of neglect. While she remained in post, she produced reports for the academic years 1915 and 1916. In July 1916 she joined the Queen Alexandra's Nursing Service as a staff nurse, serving in Egypt, Allepo in Syria and Palestine. She returned to her post in Argyll as soon as hostilities ceased and was already carrying out her prescribed duties when Patrick returned to Argyll County Council's employ in 1920.

He took up the job virtually where he had left off and was able, with the benefit of the nurse's additional statistics, to show trends in the condition of the health of school children in the county over a period of ten years. For the statistician these reports provide an invaluable source of detailed information about not only the diseases presented by the children but also their general nutritional and sanitary condition. These in turn may lead to interpretation of the general social conditions of the population during these years. Although the schools investigated were in both rural and urban locations throughout Argyll the latter can in no respect be compared with conditions in the great conurbations of the Lowlands and the towns and rural communities may therefore be taken together for purposes of discussion.

In 1913 1,683 boys were examined and 1,611 girls. Of these approximately 16 per cent were undernourished, although those in the rural areas were marginally better fed than those in the towns. A little less than 1 per cent were inadequately clothed, but 10 per cent came to school in poor footwear or none at all.

During the war years many men who had been unemployed after the failure of several of Argyll's main industries enlisted and although Army pay was not great, families enjoyed a regular income for a short while. For those who did not join the armed forces there was increased employment in agriculture and such light industry as munitions production and uniform manufacture. A number of engineers from the quarries are known to have found employment in the Clyde shipyards. Nutritional and hygiene standards in the schools showed a noticeable improvement. In her 1916 report Nurse Simpson indicated that the number of undernourished children in school had fallen to 7.5 per cent while the proportion of those ill-clothed and without adequate footwear was below 5 per cent.

Patrick resumed his yearly reports in 1921 and by 1923 he was revealing a marked decline in nutritional standards, with more than 16 per cent of children examined being undernourished while in excess of 6 per cent of children were inadequately clothed. The depression, which was to devastate the entire United Kingdom by 1926, hit first in the remote rural areas of Scotland, where unemployment figures rose rapidly from 1919 onwards.

The records indicate other interesting facets of life at the time. From 1914 to 1924 the incidence of head and body lice in school children scarcely varied at all. The condition was found in children of all class backgrounds, although it was more likely to occur in the unwashed and ill-clothed pupils. Most importantly it was the girls who presented most often with head lice, a situation which was to continue until, in the mid 1920s, the 'bobbing' of hair became fashionable and the former long, heavily dressed styles were abandoned. In 1914, 26 per cent of girls were found to have nits in their hair while only 3 per cent of boys were infested. By 1923 these figures had fallen to 10 per cent of girls and 1 per cent of boys. Boys invariably showed a greater tendency towards body lice and were more often reported to have poor hygiene standards. In 1916 nearly 5 per cent of boys were found to be infested with body lice while 2 per cent of girls were affected.

As Patrick was at pains to point out, the school medical inspections could only highlight these social problems. He felt that it was the duty of the county medical officer and the county's sanitary engineer to conduct a programme of education in health and hygiene for the adults. School teachers could be advised on methods of educating the children in health matters and were provided with suitable teaching materials for this purpose by the schools medical officer. When he eventually succeeded to the post of chief medical officer for Argyll Patrick initiated a programme of public health education which was to become a model for other counties throughout Scotland.

Such instruction was to no avail, however, if conditions at home were not improved. While many of the problems revealed were indeed the result of poverty and overcrowding, this was not the only cause for concern. There was at this time ignorance and lack of interest in matters of hygiene amongst the population generally and it took a number of major outbreaks of typhoid fever throughout the United Kingdom before the matter was properly addressed. Despite early recognition of retailing problems by Patrick and his colleagues it was not until the 1970s that the handling of food for sale to the general public was brought under control by a revised set of laws relating to food hygiene. These demanded that shop assistants serving uncooked foods to the public wear special clothing including protective polythene gloves and that there should be a strict demarcation between people and utensils used to serve cooked and uncooked meats etc.

In 1924 Patrick's old friend and mentor Dr MacNeill died in office leaving vacant the post of chief medical officer for Argyll. Although Patrick was required to put in a formal application for the position, submitting a fistful of excellent testimonials from civilian and Army colleagues alike, the job was almost certainly his from the day McNeill was buried and Patrick took over on an 'acting' basis. During the next five years Patrick was faced with the task of surveying the condition of health and welfare services in general throughout the county. He found Argyll to be in a parlous condition. There had been little movement in any sphere since the end of the war, partly because McNeill was an old man entrenched in the old ways of tackling problems but chiefly because the country generally and his own county in particular were bereft of both money and manpower. In 1929 new legislation abandoned the old parish councils and the Poor Laws and placed all welfare, including the care of the elderly and the insane, under the direct control of the chief medical officer. Patrick, as always, was in the vanguard of those ready with their proposals for reform.

In his 1929 report to the county council he put forward a major scheme for the reorganisation of all public health services. This included work with people with learning difficulties, provision for the elderly, a countywide scheme for dental-work provision and local medical facilities together with a scheme for the re-organisation of hospital facilities and ambulance services. Excluding isolation beds for communicable diseases and those set aside for the mentally ill, the county provision of hospital beds amounted to 1.6 per 1,000 head of population. In other words, there were only 100 throughout the county. There were in addition 130 beds available in Voluntary and Poor-Law hospitals, 86 of which were in poorhouse wards, all of which were poorly constructed, defective in sanitary provision and in all other respects unsuitable.★

The nursing arrangements in these places were totally inadequate, with the exception of the Lorn Combination Poorhouse in Oban where there were two trained nurses. Elsewhere, members of staff were untrained and, almost without exception, exhibited the lowest possible standards of care. In his report Patrick advocated setting aside separate institutions for the different groups requiring care. In particular he was adamant that poor people of all ages requiring medical treatment should be separated from those who were physically fit, such as senile paupers, vagabonds and those who were socially excluded because of their learning difficulties. This latter group Patrick suggested should be the responsibility of the Public Assistance Department, or, in today's language, Social Services.★★

---

★ Prior to the National Health Service, Voluntary hospitals were provided by wealthy individuals or consortia of philanthropists and supported by voluntary public subscription. Fees were charged to those who could afford them but no one was denied treatment on grounds of inability to pay. Assessment of a patient's financial resources was made by the hospital almoner, a post which disappeared at the inauguration of the National Health Service in 1948. Public Hospitals, for the destitute, elderly and insane, were financed by Local Authorities.

★★ Patrick's greatest concern was that the sick, elderly, poor and the destitute should receive proper medical treatment regardless of their ability to pay and that they should not be lumped together with vagrants or with the mentally ill in poorhouses and insane asylums. Ten years after his death the Beveridge Report laid the foundations for the Social Services and the National Health Service as you know them today. Until the reform of mental health provision which took place in the 1970s institutions for the mentally ill still contained in addition inmates who had been placed there simply because there was nowhere else for them to go. These included unmarried mothers abandoned

This was an appropriate time for a major reorganisation for another reason. Old parish boundaries, which had, in most cases, also denoted the boundaries of a particular medical practice, had often been drawn for historical rather than practical, logistical reasons. This meant that in some cases the medical officer for the parish was making long journeys to reach patients, often across water, when another MO in an adjoining parish might attend the people more easily. Patrick as chief medical officer was now in the happy position of being able to redraw the boundaries of medical practices in order to give each doctor a reasonable area to cover requiring the least possible amount of travelling across wild or watery terrain. This reform was a double-edged sword because the medical officers were now charged with a number of Local Authority responsibilities which they may or may not have had under the former parishes. In a single-doctor practice the individual medical officer would be responsible for the destitute, the mentally ill, vaccination, public health and, where appropriate, National Health Insurance services. Money formerly handed out piecemeal by the Local Authority on claims for fees submitted by the different doctors would now become part of an annual retainer fee paid to the doctor in charge of the medical practice area. In other words, the doctors would, in part, become salaried staff of the Local Authority. The larger conurbations, of which there were three in Argyll – Campbeltown, Dunoon and Oban – supported more than one medical practice. Here the Local Authority tasks would be shared by the doctors; one would be given public health and vaccination, another the destitute etc.

Once the parish had ceased to be the unit of administration, Patrick suggested the man in charge of the new medical practice area should be called

by their families, those with learning difficulties, orphans and children of poor families whose parents could not afford to keep them.

Patrick's dreams of reform were to a large extent fulfilled by the 1948 Act, although the Utopian plan was to become distorted by the retention of private medicine and by the demands of the British Medical Association. The inaugurators of the scheme, having based their calculations on data collected before 1939, grossly underestimated the demand for treatment from the general public and the service soon began to struggle to fulfil its commitments. Successive governments have attributed the extraordinary levels of debt accrued by the NHS to inefficiency of administration but should we not acknowledge that this over-expenditure is due in large part to the huge success of the enterprise. Public expectations are now so high that patients assume they will make a complete recovery from the most dire conditions and queue up for hospital treatment. In 1890 when Patrick first began to walk the wards, patients were most reluctant to enter hospital, believing it to be a last resort from which they were unlikely to emerge alive.

the Local Medical Officer (LMO) and his practice area, the Medical Service Area (MSA).

Among Patrick's many responsibilities as chief medical officer was an annual report on the viability of housing stock in the county. In this he was assisted by the council's Planning Department and the sanitation engineer, but it was for him to declare buildings unfit for human habitation. In his 1929 report on working-class accommodation in the county Patrick used criteria laid down by a London conference held in 1920 which had concluded that a proper standard of house would display the following requirements:

1) A bedroom for parents and sufficient sleeping rooms that children of different sex could sleep separately as they approached maturity.
2) Separate sanitary accommodation for each individual family.
3) An adequate supply of water for bathing and domestic purposes and a suitable supply of potable drinking water.

Using these criteria Patrick found:

1) A large number of houses which were presently unfit but which might, with little cost, be brought up to standard.
2) A number of houses requiring demolition.
3) A number of houses which were overcrowded and needed extension or replacement.

In Kintyre the figures in these three categories were as follows:

1) 119 houses would be habitable if improvements were made.
2) 3 houses required demolition.
3) 52 houses were overcrowded. In this case the families required re-housing or an extension to their present premises. He decided that 26 new dwellings of standard size were required.

By far the largest housing stock lay in the industrial villages of Lorn at Easdale, Cullipool and Balvicar and at Ballachulish, Bonawe and Furnace. Although sub-stantially built of stone under slate roofs, many of these houses were already one hundred to a hundred and fifty years old. They lacked running water and indoor sanitation and the window areas in most cases did not provide adequate daylight or ventilation. Far worse than these houses however, were the crofting houses, in particular those where the croft provided the main source of family income. Where crofters had an alternative means of employment the houses were better maintained, but, like the quarriers' cottages, they were old and lacked the basic modern amenities.

It was one thing for Patrick to point out the defects and quite another for the Local Authority to find the means of upgrading the housing. Another two decades were to pass before any serious attempt was made to improve matters. Until the mid 1950s many villages in Argyll had houses without running water or electricity and only an earth closet for sanitation.

Although his appointment as Chief Medical Officer for Argyll was in many ways the culmination of all his ambitions and gave him great pride and pleasure, Patrick was never able to attack the challenges of the job with the vigour they required. The war years, together with the trials and tribulations of being the senior figure in a large and diverse family which had experienced its own share of tragedy, now took their toll.

Always a moderately heavy smoker, the habit had taken a strong hold upon Patrick while he was in the Army and he found it difficult to operate without a substantial daily intake of nicotine. Within two years of taking up his new post he was diagnosed with a tumour of the larynx for which there was no remedy other than heroic surgery, which he refused. During the next four years Patrick's health declined to the point where he was frequently unable to get to work. His deputy, Dr C.A. Brown, records that on days when he felt too ill to board the train from Connel for Oban, he would hang a flag from his window for her to see as she passed by aboard the train on her way to work. In the evening, she would alight and take to his home any important papers needing his attention. Fortunately his new post was a desk job, necessitating his occasional attendance at meetings of the county council but otherwise requiring little or no travelling. At no time was there any formal suggestion that he should retire on grounds of ill health.

Patrick took advantage of being bound to his desk by occupying himself more and more with historical research and the preparation of articles for various learned journals. The publication of his book on Netherlorn in 1909 had resulted in an invitation to become a fellow of the Scottish Royal Society of Arts, a title which he proudly appended to all his later correspondence. By 1926 he was deeply involved with research into the life of the 1st Marquis of Breadalbane, John Campbell, who had been his father's patron and whose biography he intended to write. This required correspondence with a great many historians and legal authorities and also with the Breadalbane estate. The correspondence included an exchange of letters with the current marquis, with whom Patrick had maintained a friendly relationship throughout the war years. Another old friend, A. Scott Rankin, the artist chosen to illustrate *Netherlorn and its Neighbourhood*, also proved to be a helpful source of information.

Patrick's other absorbing interest was the progress on the Rugby football field of his son Cammie. A.C. Gillies, who was generally known as Sandy Gillies by his contemporaries, having played for the prestigious Old Watsonians Rugby Club since leaving school, was chosen in 1926 to represent Scotland, playing in the wing forward position. His prodigious kicking from any part of the field was legendary and he was capped many times during the late nineteen-twenties and early thirties, being presented to King George V at Twickenham in 1935. He was even chosen to tour South Africa with the British Lions team but was forced to decline the invitation because of his medical commitments. Patrick seems to have kept every newspaper report which mentioned his son and he filled a number of scrapbooks with cuttings.

Poor health did not deter Dr Gillies from continuing to represent his Local Authority at medical conferences around the country. In February 1930 he was due to attended one such meeting at BMA headquarters in London. Mary had gone along with him, ostensibly to do some shopping but surely to keep on eye on him. Ironically this generous man who had given his whole life to the care and comfort of the sick collapsed in his hotel bedroom and, although immediately transferred to the nearby Hallam Nursing Home, died before a doctor could be summoned to his aid. He was sixty-two years old.

Mary Gillies returned with her husband's body to his beloved Easdale, where he was interred beside his father and his son Hunter in the Kilbrandon cemetery. The list of mourners included family, friends, colleagues from government and Local Authorities nationwide and a number of his military colleagues, as well as a multitude of his former patients.

The esteem in which Patrick was held by those most closely connected with education throughout the County of Argyll is illustrated by the following extract from the minutes of the Mull School Management Committee meeting held at Aros on Friday, 20 Feb 1931: 'Those who have been associated with him as colleagues recognise his great ability and sterling character. His death has removed one of the best known and highly respected officials in the county, a capable medical officer and a sincere friend who by example and precept, has left behind him a tradition of integrity, kind consideration and sound skill

*The stone commemorating both Patrick Hunter Gillies and his son Hunter. The inscription which borders the central Celtic design is written in Gaelic.*

*Patrick's wife Mary with the family's nanny and holding Patrick's grandson, also Patrick, in 1930 or 1931.*

which will leave its mark for all time upon the County of Argyll.' From those whom he encountered during his forays into the literary world came further acclaim, as is illustrated by this passage from a letter addressed to Mary Davinia from Mr MacNaughton of the the Oban and Lorn Association, dated 3 Mar 1931: 'The history and antiquities of Argyll were unfolded to a wide and appreciative body of readers at home and abroad. His kindness of heart and his genial and interesting personality appealed to all who were privileged to know him.' Underlining the unfortunate series of delays in appointing Patrick to his last post, as chief medical officer for the county, is this comment from the honorary secretary to the North Lancashire and South Westmorland Branch of the British Medical Association: 'He was of outstanding ability and should have occupied a position of trust long before he did. It is to be regretted that he was medical officer for Argyll for so short a period of time. Men of his size are too scarce for us to afford to lose even one.'

Patrick's legacy to the nation lay not only in the services he gave to his Easdale patients and to Argyll County Council, which he served for most of his working life, but in the wisdom, experience and initiatives he brought to his military duties. All those memos and reports on all manner of subjects concerned with military medicine, not least among them the necessity for good hygiene even in the heat of battle, and his recognition that the stress of combat could cause as legitimate an injury to the mind as a gunshot could to the body, must surely have gone some way towards changing attitudes in the War Office. Far greater concern was shown in the Second World War for the general health and hygiene of the troops, and this undoubtedly enabled Britain to put a far better prepared and much healthier fighting force into the field. Only by constant argument and cajoling by such men as Patrick Gillies could such a monumental change of attitude have been brought about.

On a personal level Patrick's legacy, together with that of his brother Hugh Gillies, was the continuance of the dynasty of Gillies doctors begun in the early nineteenth century by his father Hugh and his uncle Alexander Gillies. Although Hunter failed to reach maturity, Cammie, who remained a distinguished sportsman throughout his life, turning to golf once the rugby field eluded him, went

on to become a much respected and admired medical practitioner in Macclesfield in Cheshire. His own son, Patrick, became the medical officer to one of the largest gold-mining companies in South Africa and his daughter Fiona, who as a state registered nurse and registered midwife served in a number of hospitals, became a nursing sister aboard vessels of the Union Castle line before her marriage to William Hamilton in 1982.

*P.H. Gillies' grandson, Dr Patrick Gillies, at his graduation from Edinburgh University, 1950s.*

His grandson Hunter completed his medical training at Edinburgh University at the beginning of the new millennium. Patrick's third son, Hugh, who had been so seriously impaired by his childhood accident, passed on his medical genes to his daughter Patricia who became a nursing sister, while his second daughter, Davinia, following the other family tradition of farming, spent many years in Southern Rhodesia where she and her husband, Joe Ballantyne, raised tobacco and other crops and a family of four children, two boys and two girls.

Patrick's brother Hugh, whose medical practice was in New Abbey, Kirk-cudbrightshire, fathered four children, three girls and a boy. Of these, Walter or Wattie Gillies practised medicine until his retirement, in Moffat, Dumfries and Galloway, and his daughters are both members of the medical profession. Jack Gillies, Patrick's youngest son, did not marry until a few months before his death and died without issue.

In his native village of Easdale Patrick's name is still well remembered although it is doubtful if there is anyone living today who was his patient. The older members of the community recall childhood fears of being banished to the fever hospital at Cuan and even the village children can point out the house that was once a church before it became Patrick's isolation hospital. Others remember the visits of the school nurse, testing eyesight and searching for nits with a fine-toothed comb dipped in Lysol. In the Kilbrandon churchyard the plot where many of the Gillies family are laid is dominated by an impressive obelisk to Hugh Gillies, Patrick's father. Patrick's own gravestone goes unrecognised by all except those who have the Gaelic. The elaborately decorated stone, laid flat upon the soil alongside his father's obelisk, commemorates also young Hunter Gillies who sadly never fulfilled the promise of his childhood.

Patrick Gillies touched so many lives in so many different ways that it is difficult to sum up his contribution in a few words but if one accepts Rudyard Kipling's definition of a man as one who fills each unforgiving minute with sixty seconds' worth of distance run, then Patrick Hunter Gillies was a man in every sense of the word.